PROHIBITION
. . .
IN THE
NAPA
VALLEY

PROHIBITION
...
IN THE

NAPA
VALLEY

CASTLES UNDER SIEGE

LIN WEBER

AMERICAN PALATE

Published by American Palate
A Division of The History Press
Charleston, SC 29403
www.historypress.net

Unless otherwise noted, all images are from the author's collection.

First published 2013

Manufactured in the United States

ISBN 978.1.62619.089.4

Library of Congress CIP data applied for.

To our good friend Dick Cavagnaro

He loved the Napa Valley, and the Napa Valley loved him.
—*Napa Valley Register*, July 7, 2013

CONTENTS

ACKNOWLEDGEMENTS

This has been a gratifying book to research and write. I've been collecting information on the Napa Valley in the 1920s for quite some time, and I am grateful to The History Press and editor Aubrie Koenig for giving me the opportunity to present the dark but fascinating period we call Prohibition.

Several people have been extraordinarily helpful in this project, and I would like to thank them for their generosity in sharing information about their families with me: Nichelini descendant Doug Patterson, Arrighi descendant Leslie Crenna, Hap and Patty Vasconi and the staff at Beaulieu Vineyards/Diageo, especially Will Smith, Rebecca Johnson and Curtis Graham.

I am also deeply grateful to a dear friend who passed away unexpectedly as this book was in its final stages: Dick Cavagnaro, grandson of Dave, one of Napa's most colorful bootleggers. I am dedicating this book to Dick—he'd get a kick out of that. Over the years, Dick and his wife, Carol, also a dear friend, have introduced me to many of their family members, and thanks to them I was able, several years ago, to interview Ray Cavagnaro and Ray and Gen Lawler, who remembered Prohibition days well. I was also fortunate to have the opportunity to interview several other longtime Napa Valley residents, many—but not all—of whom have since passed away. My thanks go to George Blaufus Jr., Stella Galli Raymond, Charlie Varozza, Gunilda "Jean" Rianda, Edna Gibelo, Rita Franceschi and Marsha Bettinelli. Pioneer descendant John York also possesses a wealth of information about the Napa Valley, and I am indebted to him for his assistance as well.

Italians and Italian Swiss have been profoundly important to the Napa Valley's development as a wine region. Shortly after my husband, Chris (a German Swiss), and I arrived in St. Helena in 1971, Peter Mondavi's wife, Blanche, asked me, "What do you think of Italians?" I told her I'd never thought about Italians much, but I liked gelato. (I thought I was pretty cool for knowing what gelato was back then.) She said to me, "You'd better like Italians! They're what the Napa Valley is really about." Since writing this book, I understand what she was telling me back then. Thanks, Blanche.

I would also like to extend my gratitude to the four readers who scrutinized my work and offered such a wonderful cocktail of encouragement and editorial suggestions: Mariam Hansen of the St. Helena Historical Society; Nancy Levenberg of the Napa County Historical Society; my wise and very literate friend Inger Laidley; and my dear husband, Chris, who has persevered while I have dived once again into the Napa Valley's extraordinary and compelling deep history.

Chapter 1

POETRY OR POISON?

THE EARLY TEMPERANCE MOVEMENT

Americans have been warning each other not to drink too much alcohol since colonial days. They called moderation in the consumption of intoxicating beverages "temperance," and they had good reason to admonish one another. Far from being models of sobriety, the Puritans and their colonial descendants were sloshing with alcohol much of the time. They brewed it from whatever they could get their hands on: flowers, weeds, carrots, tomatoes, apples, grapes, corn, onions and squash, among other things. Much of America's initial wealth came from trade involving slaves, sugar and rum, and the original English and northern European settlers of the eastern seaboard drank the rum in astonishingly large quantities, along with brandy, gin, wine and beer. Beer was often the beverage of choice for children, who fetched it from the brewer in bucketfuls for use at the family table. Intoxicated since youth, many colonial Americans suffered from some form of undiagnosed alcoholism themselves or from the alcoholism of their close relatives, a condition known today as "co-dependency."

After the American Revolution, when money was in short supply and the citizens were reduced to bartering, farmers in some parts of the country used whiskey as a form of currency, home-brewed from leavings of the harvest in exchange for other necessities of life. Observing this, Secretary of the Treasury

Alexander Hamilton levied a tax on alcohol, which infuriated the farmers and led to the Whiskey Rebellion of 1791–94, the first test of the United States government's willingness to enforce unpopular laws about alcohol or anything else. Taxes derived from the sale of alcoholic products have been a mainstay of the American economy since the nation's earliest days.

The problem of addiction did not go unnoticed. Founding Father Benjamin Rush, MD, wrote and lectured on the dangers of alcohol to the brains of those who drank it, although his idea of a temperance drink involved consuming a cocktail of wine and opium. The truth that some people were physiologically unable to drink moderately was not understood. An inability to "hold one's liquor" indicated, for men anyway, a lack of manliness that was to be avoided. It also suggested moral weakness. Men of good character (especially from the privileged classes), even those who staggered about most evenings, were usually not seen as having issues with alcohol unless they drained away the family resources or were caught brutalizing their wives.

Most Protestant ministers, who themselves drank, preached from the pulpit about the evils of immoderation in drink. Some of them were quite persuasive. There was nothing in the Bible about complete abstention from intoxicating beverages—a fact well known to everyone, since the Bible was standard reading for every literate man, woman and child in early America. Lyman Beecher, the father of Harriet Beecher Stowe, was a daring and ambitious preacher who felt called to do the Bible one better. He promoted the virtue of complete abstinence from alcohol and was able to attract a loyal following who felt convinced that through abstinence they were spiritually purer than their beer-swilling, rum-chugging peers. He published a popular set of six sermons on the subject of intemperance that was reprinted in several languages. It won him a good deal of recognition and provided some extra funds, which he needed in order to raise his thirteen children. Women were especially positive about Beecher's concept of abstinence, since it was they who usually suffered the consequences of their husbands' intoxication. Beecher also preached fiery sermons on the evils of the Unitarian Church, a rival for the minds and souls of New Englanders. This faith-based hate soon expanded to include Catholicism as well. His hatred of Catholicism became so infectious that after he gave a sermon on it in Boston, someone burned down the local Ursuline convent.

The early temperance movement spawned a number of splinter groups dedicated to cleaning up what many believed were their fellow countrymen's lax morals. Some, like the followers of Baptist lay preacher William Miller, combined the non-biblical call for abstinence with admonishments to observe the Jewish Sabbath (Saturday), dress modestly and obey other dicta drawn mainly and often loosely from the Old Testament. The end of the world was near, he preached, and only the morally fit (meaning sober and conservatively attired) would be chosen when Christ came again. Many permutations of the idea that temperance was a Christian necessity were spun in American churches in the mid-nineteenth century. The cloth woven from New World Protestantism and the push for abstinence from intoxicating drink would be the fabric that became the prohibition movement, as shall be seen.

Most of the people who heard these early diatribes against drink had immigrated to the New World from Britain and northern Europe. Some were from aristocratic families who maintained their Tory affiliation and moved in a small, select circle of their own. They often attended the Episcopal Church, the Americanized version of the Church of England, which was an Anglicized version of Catholicism. As in Catholicism, wine was an integral part of the Episcopalian liturgy, and sermons about ending its use altogether made no sense to them. Most Americans, however, were from the working classes. They were Congregationalists, Methodists, Presbyterians, Baptists, Quakers— "mainline" Protestants without a liturgical tradition involving wine.

With the exception of Maryland, which was Roman Catholic, all the original states were almost entirely Protestant. This demographic began to change in the 1840s, when famine and war drove emigrants from new places, especially Ireland, Germany and southern Europe. This fresh wave of newcomers included large numbers of Catholics and a much smaller number of Jews. Forced into low-paying jobs as laborers and factory workers, a common denominator among immigrants to the eastern states in the nineteenth century was poverty and all that went with it, including disease, crime, despair and the tragedy of alcoholism, which often began as an attempt to self-medicate. Lifting the glass meant lifting the spirits, literally and figuratively. Many in the traditional middle class saw only as far as the glass and believed that the poor were morally degenerate, lured into darkness by Demon Rum and, as pastor Beecher had explained, the Catholic Church.

THE GREAT ESCAPE

The year 1848 was pivotal for California, America and the globe. Until that year, California had been part of Spain and then Mexico, but when the Mexican-American War ended in February, a vast new world opened up—

one without an entrenched establishment that was steeped in East Coast tradition. Almost simultaneously, gold was discovered in the Sierra foothills, although most people were not aware of it until 1849.

This brought a massive and sudden influx of American men hoping to find their fortune in a new territory just waiting to be populated. The Gold Rush also beckoned some women of adventurous spirit, usually camp followers who provided distraction for the men. Many of these found work in San Francisco, but the Napa Valley—a popular tourist destination for the miners—also became home to many ladies of the night.

The first to gather Sierra gold were the soldiers and pioneers who were already in California when James Marshall first discovered it, although not everyone who sought it found huge amounts. One of the '48ers was Harrison Pierce, an American sailor who had jumped ship sometime around 1843 and eventually made his way to the embryonic city of Napa. With skills he had learned doing carpentry for other pioneers, he began to construct the pueblo's first commercial building, a saloon near the Napa River. Perhaps sampling too much of the inventory, Pierce and his buddy Nicholas Higuera, the original owner of the land, misread the surveyors' marks and placed it in the middle of what would become Main Street. They moved it, and just as they were starting the roof, word came that gold had been discovered in the Sierras. They dropped their hammers, joined a band of adventurers and rushed to find gold. After a few months, Pierce apparently realized that an easier way to gather gold was to collect it from the miners in exchange for booze and other pleasures. He returned to Napa, put the roof on the building and opened for business. His Empire Saloon was a hit.

Alert to a promising business opportunity, Napa pioneers Joe Chiles and Billy Baldridge built a still on Baldridge's property near what is now Yountville and provided tax-free wares for Pierce and subsequent Napa barkeeps to sell. Already admired for being among the very first to settle down in the area, Chiles and Baldridge were additionally appreciated for their whiskey. Chiles also planted grapes and may have made wine for his personal use on his remote ranch in Chiles Valley, east of what is now St. Helena.

An Englishman named John Patchett had been trained as a brewer. He bought some of Higuera's land near what are now Clay and Calistoga Streets, on which were planted mission grapes. He may have made beer at first, but he is remembered today for hiring Charles Krug to be his winemaker. Krug was a small, genial Prussian whose business partner, Agostin Haraszthy, had just started a winery in Sonoma called Buena Vista. Legend has it that Krug used a small, borrowed cider press to crush the grapes that became the first

Charles Krug made wine for commercial sale in Napa in 1858.

commercially sold wine in the Napa Valley. The site of this auspicious event was somewhere around First and Monroe Streets in Napa.

The population of early Napa Valley consisted of a blend of Americans and Europeans, with a few Mexican landowners like Higuera and, at first, several hundred Native Americans. The Indians were only a remnant of the pre-contact demographic, which had been decimated by disease in the 1820s and '30s. The native population was especially dense in what would become Rutherford and Calistoga, but it dwindled rapidly as the Caucasians made a concerted effort to drive them out. The tragic specter of emaciated, bedraggled and severely inebriated Indians watching the boat traffic at the embarcadero in Napa was common.

The Americans, who were in the majority, tended to hold the same general value system as did their counterparts back east and were very familiar with the ideas promulgated by temperance groups. The city of St. Helena—soon to become the heart of the premium wine industry—got its name when members of the local Sons of Temperance club were playing horseshoes at the blacksmith's shop, circa 1852. The little community that was forming around them needed to be called something more distinctive than Hot Springs Township, its original designation. They decided to call it St. Helena, not for the beatified mother of Constantine but for the mountain that was clearly visible to the northwest. The Sons of Temperance had already adopted the mountain's name for their group: they were the St. Helena Chapter of the Sons of Temperance. It was by no means unusual for little towns to have temperance groups. They were fraternal, mutual help associations designed to keep men manly and virtuous by drinking in moderation or not at all, and thus out of trouble with their wives. Institutions like the Sons helped preserve the values they had known back home. Like the Masons, the Sons provided help in time of sickness and funds for their members' funerals.

There was little time for California's original pioneer stratum to become a deeply rooted ruling class, because a new layer of Gold Rush hopefuls soon followed the '48ers and '49ers. In addition to huge numbers of Americans, this fresh wave of newcomers included the same mass of Catholic and Jewish immigrants that had been pouring into the cities of the East Coast. Rather than disembarking in eastern ports like New York and Boston, some of these foreign-born men (and a few women) sailed all the way to California. Jewish merchants like Freedman Levinson and his wife, Dora, who were Prussians, were instrumental in establishing commerce in every city in Napa County. The Levinsons were among the city's original Caucasian inhabitants. Their children and grandchildren became pillars of Napa society.

Anyone with the drive and desire to work hard could make a good living in California, or so it seemed. Hard work and hard play put everyone on the same level, regardless of religion or national origin, and much of the miners' social lives revolved around a shared bottle on a cold night. African Americans, who were still slaves in the southern states, drank along with them and enjoyed a degree of respect and camaraderie among the miners at the digs that was unusual for the times. With few women or preachers to nag them about the virtues of sobriety, the miners were noteworthy for their frequent lack of it. Excluded from this community were Asians and Native Americans, who were subjected to enormous amounts of harassment from Caucasian pioneers. The Asians rarely drank alcohol; their drug of choice tended to be opium. Indians were generally unable to metabolize alcohol well and became very drunk and addicted easily (thus their intoxicated presence at the embarcadero, which was near the saloons). Neither of these groups could (or perhaps even wanted to) socialize with the men who found fraternity over glasses of beer, hard liquor and, occasionally, wine.

NAPA VALLEY CITIES FORM

Because of its proximity to the gold digs and the excellent harbors in San Francisco and Oakland, Gold Rush pioneers from all parts of the world tended to settle, at first, in Northern California. Napa City was one of the earliest to develop and was associated from the very beginning of the Gold Rush with alcohol. By 1855, it had sprouted several hotels and saloons where rowdy guests could enjoy locally brewed whiskey and, in 1858, wine, thanks to Patchett and Krug and an associate winemaker, Henri Pellet, a

St. Helena's White Sulphur Springs was California's first resort.

French Swiss. An Italian named Giuseppe Migliavacca provided alcoholic beverages for locals and tourists as well, and in 1866, he built a large winery on Fifth Street at the site of today's Napa County Library. His wines may not have been the first to be fermented in Napa City, but they may have been the most popular.

As in even rowdier San Francisco, female companionship was readily available in many of Napa's hotels and their adjacent saloons, for a fee. Farther up the Napa Valley, near what soon became St. Helena, an upscale hot springs resort called White Sulphur Springs (WSS) beckoned a more elegant clientele. Here, wine was served, much of it pretty good. (Migliavacca renderings were probably well represented.)

An American doctor with Tory leanings pioneered the planting and crushing of wine grapes up valley. George Belden Crane was a New Yorker with slaveholding relatives in Alabama whose antebellum ideals he strongly supported. He constructed a small, partially subterranean wine crushing facility—nothing fancy. Crane's New York farm boy prudence outweighed

Pioneer vintner George Crane viewed wine as a cure for alcoholism. *Courtesy of Suzanne Salvestrin.*

whatever tendencies he harbored for the cavalier; nevertheless, he mingled with the guests at the Springs and served as a banker to farmers throughout the valley, keeping careful records of all his transactions. He also documented the experiments he made in his vineyard just south of St. Helena and served as a resource for other pioneer wine growers. Impressed, and eager for a steady supply of good wine for their own tables, several of the resort's wealthier patrons bought property and planted vineyards of their own. They consulted with Crane, Krug, Pellet and a few other farmers and vintners who realized that the region's volcanic soil made it uniquely suited to viticulture.

Among Crane's acquaintances were William H. Bourn and his wife, Sarah. Bourn owned the Empire Gold Mine in Grass Valley as well as the company that provided all the fresh water to the city of San Francisco. The Bourns bought acreage near the resort, where they enjoyed a reprieve from the chilly San Francisco summers. Like several of their wealthy peers, they planted grapes and lived a bit like European nobility. Their presence lured others of the same ilk, among them several retired, wine-loving Episcopalian priests.

The town of Calistoga also began as a resort. Its developer, Sam Brannan, was a Mormon who dropped his religious affiliation and became a political and financial powerhouse in the newly formed state of California. His fondness for intoxicating drink developed into full-blown alcoholism, and his drunken episodes became an embarrassment to even the hard-boiled miners. Sexual liaisons, mistreatment of employees and political chicanery further tarnished his reputation, and as a result, his resort did not find favor with people of good standing. It eventually failed.

There was plenty of public drunkenness in the Napa Valley throughout the last half of the nineteenth century. Early Napa Valley newspapers were replete

Jacob Schram hosted Robert Louis Stevenson at his winery.

with tales of mayhem rendered by people "under the influence." There was also a proliferation of wineries, as Europeans from winemaking areas and Americans with a fondness for grandeur planted vineyards and built facilities, often of stone, to crush their grapes and ferment the results. With all those miners and with all that gold dust pouring into San Francisco, the market for intoxicating beverages was quite good throughout the 1860s, '70s and much of the '80s, even though the national economy was erratic.

The famous author Robert Louis Stevenson and his bride, Fanny, passed through Calistoga on their honeymoon. Stevenson loved wine and worried that it might some day "withdraw its poetic countenance" from the dinner table because of infestation problems in the vineyards of France. They were typical of the small class of upscale Anglo-Saxon consumers who liked wine with their meals and drank without becoming inebriated. They stopped off for a wine tasting at the home/vineyard/winery of vintner Jacob Schram, a German, who poured glass after glass of his wares to the somewhat overwhelmed author. Stevenson called California wine "experimental" and lamented that it was drunk before it had time to age—his wry way of suggesting that unpracticed California vintners like Schram drank too much of it too soon, too often.

OHIO

While California was welcoming newcomers of all social classes, the majority back east grew increasingly xenophobic. As the nineteenth century progressed, never-ending shiploads of foreign-born people were deposited in Boston, New York and New Orleans. For these transplanted masses, neighborhood saloons served as gathering places, meeting halls and the source of a free lunch. Established citizens learned to avoid these sections of the city, calling them "slums." It was usually in such places that prostitution was available, a service that gentlemen from the more proper neighborhoods often utilized. The sex trade was hard for many in the Victorian period to discuss, so complaints about the squalid parts of town centered most often on the saloons and their inebriated clientele, and little was said about prostitution. The two often came together, however, underlining the notion that alcohol and morality were at odds with each other and that cities were suspect places, while rural settings were healthy and wholesome. (It is a perception that lingers today, despite fables like that of the city mouse and the country mouse, which portray the dangers lurking in each.)

Much as it abhorred the stench and corruption of the slums and saloons, the East Coast middle class was not responsible for what eventually became the prohibition movement. The action in the battle to ban liquor altogether began in Ohio. Ohio was a major producer of intoxicating beverages. By the 1860s, it was fermenting more wine than any other state, including California. The tradition waned because of the Civil War, but in the 1880s, the old art returned, thanks in part to the addition of German immigrants. It had a large Jewish population as well. Many Jews had been in the wine and hard liquor business in Europe. The B. Manischewitz Company, for example, was founded by a rabbi (Rabbi Dov Behr Manischewitz) in Cincinnati, although it later moved its headquarters to New York State. Breweries were also big business in Ohio. First-generation Irish, Italian and German immigrants in Ohio suffered the same problems they did on the eastern seaboard: poverty and the miseries that accompanied it. Beer, wine and hard liquor were part of their culture, and they often enjoyed them in saloons, particularly in the suburbs just outside Columbus, the capital. It was in the heartland state of Ohio that the leap from temperance to abstention became politicized and here that abstention merged with another phenomenon: faith-based hate.

East Coast preacher Lyman Beecher helped to fuel that leap. In 1832, he accepted the presidency of a seminary near Cincinnati, where he readied young ministers to win the West for his brand of Christianity. His published works about temperance had brought him fame and at least modest wealth. Upping the ante from temperance to abstinence only increased his popularity, especially among women. The two great evils, he preached, were alcohol and Catholicism. (Unitarianism, the other religion he hated, was not significant in Ohio.) His students in Ohio held tightly to Beecher's faith-based hate and abhorrence of intoxicating beverages long after he returned to the East Coast, where he eventually faced charges of heresy. His Ohio protégés let his ideas ferment and passed them on to others.

St. Helena wine pioneer George Crane was living in Ohio during Beecher's stay there. He joined the Sons of Temperance in Scioto County and signed a pledge to give up whiskey. He observed that because it was cheap, whiskey was the main alcoholic beverage in use because (as he wrote in his *Memoirs*) "but a few men could afford to dissipate on costlier liquor" like wine and brandy. While many signed the pledge, few of the Ohioans he knew could tolerate the complete absence of alcohol, especially when they saw wealthy Sons members enjoying wine. "The poor," he wrote, "grew jealous of the baneful blessing." The idea of total abstinence from all alcohol of any kind was seen as a social equalizer, but it was very difficult to achieve when others were sipping wine with no apparent harm.

One who used Lyman Beecher's ideas to augment his own fame was a fake doctor named Diocletian Lewis, who, among other things, claimed to be able to cure tuberculosis. His remedies didn't work, but they were lucrative. During the Civil War, he ran a girls' school in Massachusetts, where he met Catharine Beecher, one of Lyman's daughters. Lewis was a persuasive orator. He acquired a group of devoted female followers and hit upon the idea of an ongoing lecture called "The Duty of Christian Women in the Cause of Temperance." He instructed women to confront shopkeepers who sold alcohol and demand that they sign a pledge vowing to stop. If they refused, the women should pray and sing hymns until the shopkeepers obeyed.

Lewis's lecture circuit brought him to Ohio in 1873. Although open to innovation and social justice in some ways (many Ohioans had been ardent abolitionists), most in the Ohioan old guard were not prepared to assimilate the foreign-born, African American and otherwise non-mainline newcomers who flowed into Ohio after the Civil War—especially drinking ones. Having already linked together religion and alcohol, many were rapt by Lewis's oratory.

Eliza Jane Trimble Thompson, daughter of a twice-elected Ohio governor and wife of a prominent judge, was especially entranced with him. Fierce in her opposition to saloons, "Mother Thompson" synthesized the concept that the consumption of alcohol was a spiritual problem that required a spiritual cure. She organized bands of like-minded local women to stand outside the businesses of selected local merchants and sing and pray them into suspending their alcohol sales. These "Women's Crusades" spread across Ohio and into twenty-two other states. The stores resumed their customary business after a few days, but the women had made their point. (Diocletian

Lewis tried to take credit for the Crusades' brief but stunning success, but historians usually point to Mother Thompson as their inspiration.)

In 1874, the Second Presbyterian Church in Cleveland, Ohio, girded its loins to host the invocation for a holy war against "strong drink." Women from eighteen states gathered there for three days in November to form something they called the National Woman's Christian Temperance Union (WCTU), sponsored by Wheaton College of Illinois. The WCTU's purpose was to combat the influence of alcohol on families and society. With the same reformist zeal that had infused their abolitionist parents, these women promoted "temperance in all things healthful" and "total abstinence from all things harmful," with the understanding that alcohol in any quantity at all was poisonous.

Having cut her teeth in a leadership role with a local chapter, a dynamic woman named Frances "Frank" Willard left her post as dean of women at Northwestern University to take the helm of the National WCTU. She devoted her all to the promulgation of social justice as she saw it. The main theme of her ideology was that women needed to become politically empowered and to use that energy to overthrow the repressive and denigrating behaviors of men, among which was their proclivity for alcohol and their consumption of it in saloons. She wove together the concepts of women's suffrage and temperance, which to her meant prohibiting alcohol altogether by means of legislation. She saw the election ballot as the best way for women to protect their homes from "the legalized traffic in strong drink."

In addition to her rejection of men, Frank harbored a deep distaste for recent immigrants, who brought with them, she felt, their loathsome Catholicism and their fondness for alcohol. She lobbied Congress to pass anti-immigration measures to keep out what she called "the scum of the old world." She advocated a full court press to accomplish these goals. Her slogan was "Do Everything," which meant lobbying, preaching, writing and educating to bring about the societal changes she had in mind. By the time she died in 1898, she had seen to it that the WCTU had well-organized chapters in every state and, equally importantly, that WCTU principles involving abstention from alcohol had gotten into the curriculum of American public schools.

The WCTU's triumphs in the field of education were largely the work of Mary Hanchett Hunt of Massachusetts. By the time schoolchildren of the 1870s and '80s became adults, many of them were fully inculcated with WCTU ideals, which they passed along to their own children as givens. Hunt strongly believed that alcohol of any kind in any amount is unhealthy for all people. This questionable premise appeared as fact in school textbooks, thanks to Hunt, who "officially" endorsed pedagogical materials that promoted temperance with so-called scientific information about alcohol. This included such dicta as the idea that swallowing liquor would forever scorch the throat and that all beer drinkers eventually died of dropsy. In her writings and no doubt her personal life, Hunt castigated immigrants ("these immigrant hordes," she called them) almost as vigorously as she attacked alcohol.

Firebrand Susan B. Anthony began her political career as a strong temperance advocate. She founded the Daughters of Temperance because the Sons of Temperance forbade women to speak at their meetings. Similar exclusions drove temperance's would-be female leadership into taking up a parallel cause: women's suffrage. It was men, not women, who spent their pay in saloons, beat their spouses and drove their families to destitution. Men could not be trusted, the suffragettes believed, to govern themselves, and laws needed to be on the books to prevent their evil ways. As a result, gifted women like Anthony, Amelia Bloomer and Lucy Stone turned from the temperance movement and put their energy into getting women the right to vote. Once that occurred, they reasoned, legislating morals would be a cinch. Frances Willard, however, continued to focus on temperance.

Willard lived to see the formation of the Anti-Saloon League (ASL). It was created in 1895, also in Ohio. Its titular head was a Methodist minister named Purley Baker, but the real brains behind the ASL belonged to a small, natty Ohioan with a neatly trimmed mustache: Wayne Wheeler. His mission was to get into public office candidates who were "Dry"—that is, who promoted not just moderation but total abstinence from alcohol. Working from inside the state and federal government, these hand-chosen representatives would, Wheeler believed, use the full force of the law to close down the alcoholic beverage industry.

How could he cause men to trade their saloons for a life of sobriety? He couldn't, he reasoned, but their wives could. Wheeler saw the logic in appealing to women as a force for change. Like Lyman Beecher and Diocletian Lewis, he knew where to find them: in Protestant churches, where they worshipped, volunteered, socialized and formed their opinions based on the sermons of their ministers. Once in his grasp, women would be the tools who would leverage the prohibition of alcohol.

Chapter 2

BOOM AND BUST IN THE NAPA VALLEY

CASTLES

Like Charles Krug and George Belden Crane, Gottlob Groezinger and his wife, Elisabeth, were pioneers of the California wine industry. Born in Germany in 1820, they arrived in the United States in 1856, while they and the Gold Rush were both in their prime. Gottlob was a small man with dark hair, a heavy German accent and a taste for fine food and wine that he had cultivated while working as a waiter in Switzerland. He opened a wine shop at Pine and Battery in San Francisco, and by 1870, he had collected enough of the miners' gold dust to buy vineyard land in Yountville in the Napa Valley. The Groezingers knew that supplying their own product would assure them of profits. Once they had established the name Groezinger in the lucrative alcohol beverage trade, they could found a dynasty like the ones in France and Germany.

Having grown up in the shadow of castles in Europe, the Groezingers thought in grand terms. They built an elaborate, 400,000-gallon-capacity brick winery and a distillery. To ensure water for their enterprise, they dug four reservoirs in the nearby western hills and put down pipes to direct a year-round stream into Hopper Creek and down the hill toward their facility. For the winery's convenience, a spur of the Southern Pacific Railroad led directly to their door. They made wine and brandy in Yountville and provided the grapes for a champagne producer in San Francisco, Alois Finke. When Finke died in 1874 (the same year the WCTU was founded), the Groezingers took over his business, calling it A. Finke's Widow.

For at least part of the time, Gottlob remained in San Francisco while Elisabeth lived in Yountville, where she managed and provided lodging for at least twenty men, presumably employees, almost all of them recent European immigrants. The Groezingers' operation was huge for its day, and it is clear that both Gottlob and Elisabeth had their hands full.

All went well with the Groezingers for several years, but as the 1870s melted into the 1880s, strange things started happening to their vines. The leaves began to curl up long before autumn, and the grapes turned into raisins before they ripened. Their neighbor, pioneer grape grower Green Whitton, saw the same thing happening to his vines, as well. At first Whitton and others attributed the shriveling of their vines to the strong wind that often blew through the area, but eventually the true cause was discovered. A plague of tiny root lice called phylloxera had invaded the root systems of premium wine grapes. They slowly killed the vines by forming nodes inside of which they sucked juices from the roots while strangling them. The plague first showed up near Yountville. As it turned out, it was the same problem that had decimated the vineyards of France, causing Stevenson to fear for the future of viticulture. Eventually, the insects found their way into nearly every vineyard in the valley, and growers frantically sought a cure. The 1880s were a time of economic boom, so the market for high-quality wine was positive. The Groezingers replanted and helped San Franciscans drink to the good times. Even if the grapevines didn't produce as well as they had hoped, they still had their retail stores.

A few miles north of Groezinger's up the dusty, rutted cart path that served as the county road, there was another pioneer winery: To Kalon, the fine enterprise of H.W. Crabb. Its Greek name (meaning "the highest good") hinted that its owner had been graced with a classical education and therefore possessed a degree of wealth. Arriving in Napa shortly after the Civil War, Crabb invested his time, energy and fortune into developing and growing grape varieties that suited the climate and soil in his part of the valley. His wines won prizes in international competitions, and he did much to further the area's reputation as a premium wine-growing region. The small community of Oakville sprang up around a train station that the Southern Pacific Railroad built especially for Crabb's use. This could have resulted in the little whistle stop getting the name "Crabb," but instead it was called "Oakville," named for a magnificent tree on the other side of the county road. Crabb's winery was

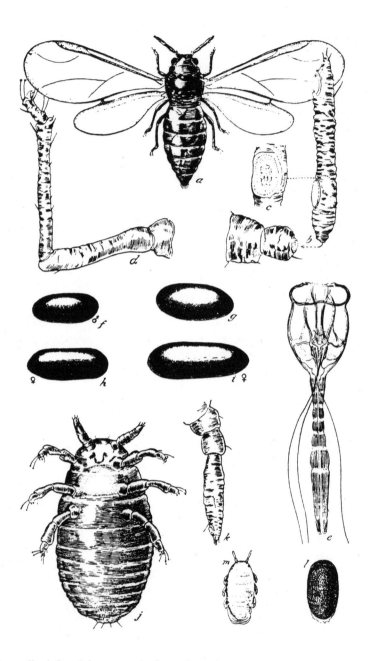

Phylloxera lice infested the rootstock of premium wine grapes.

H.W. Crabb's To Kalon winery was Oakville's first significant winery. *Courtesy of the Napa Valley Wine Library Association.*

a big wooden building painted red, like a barn in the Ohio wine country where he was born and raised. The phylloxera nestled into Crabb's fine vineyard, too. He replanted, but his funds were exhausted. The little lice forced him to borrow from the Goodman Bank in Napa.

Crabb's neighbor was John Benson, a former San Francisco real estate magnate. He also had a train stop of his own, which was called simply Benson. He put in a vineyard and built a massive, castle-like winery he called Far Niente, from the Italian phrase *dolce far niente*: "sweet to do nothing." He was *far niente* about acquiring a permit to make and sell wine and about paying the requisite tax on it as well. Federal tax agents were not *dolce* about this, even though Benson was wealthy and powerful. They placed three men in charge of monitoring his alcohol-related activities: his friend H.W. Crabb, his foreman Andrew Hansen and Melchior Kemper, the owner of the Oakville Mercantile store across from the depot. It is highly unlikely that any of the three exercised diligence as proxies for the Treasury Department.

John Benson imagined himself royalty in his retirement villa, Far Niente. He also made wine. *Courtesy of the Napa Valley Wine Library Association.*

Hamden McIntyre got his start at Gustav Niebaum's Inglenook Winery, which he designed. *Courtesy of the Napa Valley Wine Library Association.*

There was another train stop just a couple miles up the road from Crabb and Benson: Rutherford, which by 1880 was already home to an expanse of vineyard land. Serranus Clinton Hastings, first chief justice of the California Supreme Court and founder of the Hastings Law School in San Francisco, grew grapes on his vast acreage there in the 1860s and donated the land for an east–west road that terminated at the station. The other end wound up into the eastern hills, finally terminating in Pope Valley. For a while, people called it the Hastings-Rutherford Road, but after Hastings sold much of his vineyard and withdrew from the wine business, it became known as the Rutherford Cross Road.

William C. Watson, cashier of the Bank of Napa, acquired seventy acres just west of Hastings's, against the western foothills, which he called Inglenook. He lavished his estate not only with plantings of foreign and domestic grapes but also with whimsical enhancements like a fully stocked trout stream and a hand-dug swimming hole with a diving board. He seems to have envisioned Inglenook as a destination resort, similar to White Sulphur Springs. Phylloxera, storm damage and the competition from WSS, Calistoga and other Napa Valley resorts may have reduced his profit margin. He sold out to a Finnish sea captain with a brilliant mind for business, Gustav Niebaum, who retired from his fabulously successful career on the ocean to enjoy life in a sea of grapevines. Niebaum hired as his winemaker a New Yorker who was as multitalented and meticulous as he was: Hamden McIntyre.

Engineer, chemist, artist and architect, McIntyre liked the concept of "gravity flow," where the grapes were introduced to the press on the top floor of the winery and the juice poured down into fermenters below. To achieve this, the winery needed to be at least two stories tall, with plenty of room for fermentation and storage tanks, which meant that the winery had to be quite large. McIntyre had already been the architect for Far Niente, as well as the much less imposing wooden winery of a German vintner named Christian Adamson in Rutherford. Niebaum wanted Inglenook to appear at least as grand as Benson's place. The chateau-like Inglenook took about five years to complete. McIntyre had a hand in building several other grand buildings in the wine industry in the final two decades of the nineteenth century, among them Beaulieu, Greystone, Hedgeside and Eshcol (today's Trefethen). His huge, stately structures, most of them hewn from local stone, helped change the appearance of the Napa Valley from a typical Northern California agricultural zone to an oasis of European culture where castles stood watch over carpets of green.

Eshcol Winery was another McIntyre creation.

Lots of the action in the early wine industry was taking place in St. Helena. In addition to Crane's contribution, much of the upper valley's development as an early nexus of wineries was due to the hard work and personal appeal of the Prussian Charles Krug, who moved there after his marriage to Caroline Bale in 1860. Caroline was the daughter of the recipient of a huge Mexican land grant in the upper Napa Valley around St. Helena. Krug planted as much of her inheritance as he could in premium grapevines. He observed them carefully and shared his thoughts on viticulture with other wine growers. He, too, built a large, handsome stone winery.

The phylloxera bugs had a feast on the roots of Krug's cherished vines. Without retail stores to buttress his income, Krug experienced scarcity in the midst of plenty. Caroline was besieged with bouts of depression and was finally committed to the state-run mental hospital in Napa, where she died. (It's possible that alcohol was at the root of Caroline Krug's suffering. Her father had a serious and notorious alcohol habit; genetics are now known to play a part in the development of alcoholism.)

Charles Krug himself passed away in 1892, broke. James K. Moffitt, a businessman who was a regent of the University of California, bought the Krug estate and lived on it at least part of the time. He leased out the winery to Krug's nephew, Bismarck Bruck, who managed the production of wine there.

Another Prussian, William Scheffler, also had large holdings of land in St. Helena. In 1880, he bought an existing winery, Edge Hill, from the suicidally depressed son of a former general in the Mexican-American War, Richard Heath. He poured money into its beautification (it, too, resembled a small castle) and installed a private waterworks. He also built a distillery, which was useful for reprocessing inferior wine into brandy. He bought up acres of bug-ridden vineyards and in 1885 purchased the old White Sulphur Springs resort, perhaps hoping to attract a wealthy clientele to his wines and brandies. When this failed, he tried to borrow from anyone and everyone, including the domestic help of his San Francisco friends, who could ill afford investing in vineyards, especially infested ones. He left St. Helena and moved to San Francisco, where the city directory listed him as being in the liquor business. He died in 1893.

Having a lot of money to begin with was very helpful if a winery were to rise to the challenges of farming. Alfred Loving Tubbs had made buckets of it selling ropes during the Gold Rush. He spent some of it on summers at White Sulphur Springs, and in 1882, he bought 254 acres near Calistoga at the foot of Mount St. Helena. His winery, Chateau Montelena, looked very much like a castle, complete with turrets and battlements. It became one of the largest wine producers in the valley.

Another man with deep financial resources was Charles Carpy, who owned the Uncle Sam Winery in downtown Napa. He was also president of the French American Bank in San Francisco and had a winery in San Jose. Born in Bordeaux, he had friends and helpful connections in San Francisco's French district—people who enjoyed wine and drank it regularly. His wines were popular in New Orleans, as were the offerings of two Oakville vintners, Adolph Brun and Jean Chaix, proprietors of Nouveau Medoc, across the road from Crabb's place. With a dedicated group of consumers—the wine-loving French—Carpy and the Nouveau Medoc owners prospered where others failed.

In 1893, Carpy added another winery to his collection: Greystone, the site of today's Culinary Institute of America, the enormous stone building between St. Helena and Calistoga. Greystone's original owners were Sarah Bourn and her children, the wealthy friends of George Crane. (William

Above: Greystone Winery between St. Helena and Calistoga was the largest in the state.

Opposite, top: The Tubbs winery in Calistoga was designed to resemble a castle.

Opposite, bottom: Brun and Chaix's Nouveau Medoc Winery, founded in the 1870s, became known as the French-American Wine Company.

Bourn, the goldmine owner, had died as a result of accidentally severing an artery while shaving.) The winery was another palatial creation of McIntyre's and was thought to be the largest in California at that time.

THE BURSTING BUBBLE

By 1889, there were 142 wineries in Napa County, with twenty-five thousand acres planted in grapes. The good times of the 1880s, however, had been based on a bubble. When it popped in 1893, several key industries—railroads and mining companies in particular—were over-extended and suffered the consequences. Investors panicked, and a sharp, nationwide recession ensued. At its worst, national unemployment may have exceeded 15 percent. This did nothing to ease the plight of the continuing flood of European immigrants still streaming into East Coast cities. Slums proliferated as wealthier families fled from increasingly overpopulated urban centers and established new homes in former farm- and pastureland called suburbs, made possible by improvements in transportation, especially commuter trains and bridges.

The Panic of 1893 was a frightening experience for many sectors of the nation. Wealthy, non-immigrant Americans who had not grown up in wine-drinking cultures became more frugal with their money; practically overnight, the market for high-end alcoholic beverages became thin. The year 1894 was a nightmare for wine growers and vintners.

The vagaries of the final decade of the century wreaked havoc on H.W. Crabb's once ample bank account, and he was forced to borrow again. He rang up considerable debt with the Goodman Bank, and when he passed away in 1899, he owed more than his net worth. To Kalon went up for auction on the courthouse steps. An executive at Goodman named Edward Churchill walked away with the title to the property.

Churchill was one of Napa City's most important movers and shakers during the second half of the nineteenth century. He came to Napa in 1878 to join the cousins of his wife Mary: James and George Goodman, who had started the city's first bank. The bank prospered along with the town, and the cousins enjoyed sumptuous lifestyles in mansions that still stand in Napa's historic district. (Churchill Manor, for example, has ten thousand square feet of museum-quality interior space with columns, a grand staircase and twelve-foot-high ceilings.) In addition to serving as cashier of the bank, Churchill owned a Napa brewery called Golden Ribbon. The Churchills took over Crabb's winery. This did not go over well with some in Oakville, especially those who had endured the same frustrations of phylloxera and the failing economy that Crabb had seen. The senior Edward may not have cared whether Oakvillans liked him or not, but his years as a winery owner proved to be limited. In 1903, he accidentally poisoned himself by drinking carbolic acid and died before he could reach the hospital. His survivors continued to operate To Kalon.

Elisabeth Groezinger grew ill and died in 1895. Shortly afterward, Gottlob put the Yountville estate on the market, but there were no takers at first for the big brick buildings and related structures. He sold a portion of his interest to another vintner, but the facility languished and the winery went bankrupt. The family decided to break up the property into small parcels and sell it piece by piece. Much of what is today's town of Yountville stands on what was once the Groezingers' failed little empire.

Most if not all of the Napa Valley wine industry pioneers saw their bank accounts shrink because of the phylloxera epidemic. Quite a few died in the 1890s, their deaths perhaps hastened by stress and in some

Fritz Rosenbaum poured thousands of dollars into beautifying his Johannaberg home/winery. *Courtesy of Alexandra Haslip.*

cases by over-self-medicating with too much of their wares (or operating clumsily while under the influence). But because the vintners appeared to be people of worth with excellent social skills, their fellow Californians rarely accused them of moral lassitude.

Fritz Rosenbaum, a Reform Jew from a small German town near Hamelin, was one who included his wife and six children in his winery operation, which was located between St. Helena and Calistoga on what is now Highway 29 (site of today's St. Clement Winery). He financed his winemaking enterprise with the proceeds from his glass and mirror company in San Francisco at 421 Battery Street. Unlike the Groezingers, who invested their funds in vineyard acreage, the Rosenbaums poured money into the beauty of their estate. They called their mansion Johannaberg, for Fritz's wife Johanna, and it eventually overlooked a sea of green vines that included his own small vineyard and the expanse of green that was Krug's. He made thousands of gallons of wine, but there is no evidence that he sold any of it. Phylloxera found his hillside property, and he replaced his vines with more of the same kind, which they also sucked dry. Meanwhile, he poured money into his shop in the city, which continued to thrive. His was among the first businesses in San Francisco to install a telephone.

He crushed his grapes in his backyard and stored the fermenting product in the basement at Johannaberg, which proved to be a redolent temptation for his sons. Fred Jr., the older boy, developed an incorrigible anger problem, enflamed by alcohol. Young August was a full-blown alcoholic by the time he was twenty. As the disease progressed, August developed tremors and underwent episodes of paranoia. One hot September day in 1889, after proclaiming that someone wanted to kill him, August wandered away from home and disappeared. A search party scoured the area for him, and a bulletin went out alerting police in San Francisco to be on the lookout. His decomposing body was found five days later in the brush not far from a local whorehouse (more on that later) near St. Helena's Pope Street Bridge. The newspaper attributed his death to "exhaustion."

Not long after, Johanna Rosenbaum developed cancer. She died in December 1891 at the age of only forty-eight, and on New Year's Day 1892, Fritz and the remaining children received her body at the train station near their home. Fritz preferred the city, so Johannaberg went to seed. So, tragically, did Fritz. His resources quickly depleting, he drank until his liver and his mind both failed. He spent his remaining weeks in the German Hospital in San Francisco and died in November 1902 of cirrhosis of the liver and dementia. The words "alcoholic," "alcoholism" and "addiction," though known, were rarely applied to likable persons like Fritz Rosenbaum.

Planting, replanting and building well-appointed mansions appealed to men and women of European origin, where the extravagances of the wine-loving aristocracy had left their marks on the landscape for hundreds of years. American-born farmers may not have fallen into delusions of grandeur as readily (although some Napa bankers apparently did). When it was clear that phylloxera had the upper hand, many of them gave up the wine business altogether and planted prunes and walnuts. Fruit dryers went up where grapevines had been. Some who had once been involved in the wine industry feared the damage that alcohol abuse could do and sold out, breaking their estates into smaller parcels. Many moved to Southern California, helping to trigger a population explosion there.

Among those who questioned their involvement in the alcoholic beverage industry was wine pioneer George Crane, who appears to have battled depression in his later years. Shortly after his sixteen-year-old grandson George committed suicide, the aging Crane consulted a psychic, who said she had made contact with the boy in the great beyond and that young George had dictated a message for her to give grandpa. It appeared on a piece of slate. (At first she tried to imply that the boy himself had written it through automatic writing, but a handwriting expert confirmed that the handwriting was hers.) Younger George apologized for lacking "moral courage to face the consequences of my intemperance." The medium revealed that little George had consumed two beers before his death. After mulling this over, the credulous Crane considered his own inconsistency about using alcoholic products. In his *Memoirs*, he wrote, "Total abstinence from all intoxicants interdicts the use of wine drinking, and grandpa, while discouraging its use, is helping to flood the country with wine." His solution to this apparent hypocrisy was one that the wine industry would later employ in its fight against prohibition: that drinking "pure" wine (= non-adulterated wine) would actually reduce the amount of intoxication nationwide. This rationale followed a line of reasoning that Thomas Jefferson used in a letter after his presidency: "No nation is drunken where wine is cheap; and none sober where the dearness of wine substitutes ardent spirits as the common beverage. It is, in truth, the only antidote to the bane of whisky."

That alcohol caused some but not others to become addicted continued to mystify everyone. In addition to citing moral weakness as the root of alcoholism, Crane and many in the wine business believed that wine could actually be a cure for intemperance. (It isn't.) Finding a cure for phylloxera turned out to be quite a bit easier than finding one for addiction. It consisted of grafting premium varieties onto roots of vines that were more bug resistant. With this change in the vineyards, things began to turn around.

Recovery

The wine industry recovered from both phylloxera and the financial panic, and those who had remained in the vineyard business and had grapes to sell did well, because with the supply down, the price of grapes was good. This was hard on vintners who lacked significant vineyards of their own and had to pay top prices in order to have anything to sell. Many small, independent wineries became extinct or were bought by a new player in the industry: the California Wine Association (CWA).

The California Wine Association built an immense facility in Richmond after the 1906 earthquake.

The CWA was a wine trust organized in 1894 by seven of the state's largest wine merchants, all operating in San Francisco. Like Charles Carpy, one of the principal founders, most of them had vineyards themselves that supplied at least some of the wine they sold. The CWA built an enormous crushing, bottling and storage facility in San Francisco that would come to a crashing and fiery end a few years hence. The CWA blended wines carefully and sold them with labels proudly advertising Calwa wines. The CWA could afford to pay growers more money than the few remaining independent wineries could. Many Napa Valley wineries (among them Greystone and Nouveau Medoc) thus sold out to the wine trust.

The CWA blended its wines from numerous vineyards throughout the state and sold it all in bottles. This resolved two of the California wine industry's most troubling problems: lack of consistent quality and lack of customer loyalty. In the past, most California wine had been conveyed to its final destination in barrels. Much could go wrong, causing it to spoil. It was often served in pitchers, so few who ordered it in restaurants knew exactly where it came from. Because California wine was considered inferior to European offerings, it was frequently decanted into bottles with misleading or untruthful labels and sold for more than its worth. During his trip west, Robert Louis Stevenson visited a wine merchant in San Francisco who kept a drawer full of such wine labels, most of them referencing castles in Spain, which he could affix to bottles containing California wine. No laws were in place to prevent this fraud.

A far more sinister fraud also involved the wine industry, although not in California. Bogus winemakers were known to have concocted a brew they passed off as wine that had never seen a grape. The ingredients included such things as molasses, water, rum, logwood (a dye, aka brazilwood) and lead acetate, a sweet-tasting but poisonous derivative of lead that dissolved in water and served as a fixative for the dye. In the minds of many, ordering a glass of wine was tantamount to ordering a glass of poison.

The failure of independent wineries and the fracturing of large vineyard holdings into smaller parcels opened the door to a new generation of would-be Napa Valley vintners and grape growers. This new layer of wine lovers operated on a shoestring at first but usually had enough money to bug-proof their investment by grafting premium varietals onto phylloxera-resistant rootstock. The overwhelming majority of this second generation in the wine industry was foreign-born and Catholic, and they streamed into the Napa Valley around the turn of the twentieth century.

MORE EUROPEANS

As it had done since the Gold Rush, the Napa Valley offered new hope and new opportunities to those who could work hard. The wine industry gave these European families a chance they would not have found in many places in America.

In Rutherford, for example, Georges de Latour, a Frenchman, bought Frederick Ewer's big stone winery after his own small wooden one across the street burned down. He changed its name from Valley View Winery to Beaulieu. He began modestly, by starting a cream of tartar works and selling the results, mainly for use in cooking. (Cream of tartar is produced from the tartrates that collect in wooden wine barrels as the wine ages.) He imported French rootstock that was resistant to phylloxera, bought up land near the original winery at low prices and replanted. A Catholic, de Latour felt a sense of commitment to causes promoting social justice, especially Catholic ones. When the Archdiocese of San Francisco decided to install a boys' orphanage on acreage it owned in Rutherford, de Latour agreed to introduce its young charges to viticulture. It replaced a prison farm where inmates sometimes escaped, frightening the residents. Country life,

Above: The Ewer Atkinson Winery was predecessor to Beaulieu.

Left: Georges de Latour. *Courtesy of Diageo North America.*

most people agreed, was healthier for children than running about on city streets. A ramification of this decision would prove at least as helpful to de Latour as it was to the boys themselves. De Latour became fast friends with San Francisco archbishop Patrick William Riordan and had two Catholic clergymen on the board of directors of his winery. In 1912, the archbishop wrote de Latour a letter of introduction to Catholic clergy on the East Coast, where the amiable Rutherford vintner planned to make a trip to market altar wines. He established an office in New York and made important contacts in other cities, especially the heavily French New Orleans.

De Latour was French, but the majority of this next group of new immigrants to the Napa Valley was Italian and Italian Swiss, Catholic refugees from the rocky, ruggedly beautiful southern slopes of the Alps. Once controlled by Austrian Hapsburgs, that region had suffered political and climate setbacks that sent a large portion of its population seeking new lives elsewhere. Among those to leave was Battista Salmina, who had gone to work in the 1860s for his cousin Frank, a dairy farmer in the Yountville area. Battista was able to accumulate enough money to return to Switzerland, marry his young niece Sabina and return with her to the Napa Valley in the 1870s. (Intermarriage with relatives was not unusual in remote Alpine valleys at that time.)

Young Sabina was homesick, and life on Frank's dairy farm was miserable for her, so around 1880, Battista bought a hotel/saloon in St. Helena near the corner of Spring Street and Oak Avenue to provide her with companionship and cheer her up. He named it the William Tell after the legendary Swiss hero who had challenged an Austrian overlord. He also invited Sabina's brother Felix and his family to join them there. Both Salmina families lived on the second floor of the hotel while patrons gathered at the saloon below, drank wine and beer and speculated in their native tongues about the temperance movement back east and the future of the alcoholic beverage industry. Felix left barkeeping to learn winemaking, and in 1895, he was able to buy a distressed winery located near Calistoga called Larkmead. Felix and Battista entered the venture together, with Felix at the winery while Battista remained at the William Tell.

As the century turned, more and more Italians and Swiss found their way to the bar and to another favorite watering place in St. Helena, the Europa Hotel. For a time, Luigi Vasconi, Antonio Forni and Gaetano Rossi owned the Europa jointly. They were all from Northern Italy and arrived in the Napa Valley before the turn of the twentieth century. Luigi went on to work for the newly created Italian Swiss Colony wine company in Asti and eventually became the foreman/superintendent there. Antonio remained in St. Helena with his wife, Mariana Tosetti Forni, their three children and Mariana's mother in a home on the corner of Oak and Madrona Avenues, close enough for Antonio to walk to work. Barkeeping was not Antonio's ambition, however. He saved his earnings, and when the real estate market was especially favorable, he was

Left: Multitalented Gaetano Rossi was a leader in the up-valley Italian community. *Courtesy of Leslie Crenna.*

Opposite, top: Spring Street, St. Helena, circa 1900. The Europa Saloon and the Wilhelm Tell attracted Italians and Italian Swiss. *Courtesy of the St. Helena Historical Society.*

Opposite, bottom: The brewery was popular with everyone. *Courtesy of the St. Helena Historical Society.*

able to purchase some farmland north of town. He bought phylloxera-infested acreage and a decrepit winery from a pioneer female vintner named Josephine Tychson (site of today's Freemark Abbey).

Ted Arrighi, a winemaker/vineyardist who lived on or very near the Tychson property, served as Tychson's foreman. He was Luiza Vasconi's brother. Ted and Antonio planted bug-resistant vines, but that was the easy part. The Fornis and Arrighis would be proud to have an impressive, well-built stone winery like the fine, sturdy structures back home. They would honor their Italian ancestry by calling it the Lombarda Winery.

Luigi Vasconi passed away in 1900, and his widow, Luiza, returned to St. Helena with her sons Joseph, Louis and Mario and her daughter Margaret. She bought a house on Madrona Avenue, near the Fornis. (According to the U.S. Census that year, fourteen-year-old Joseph Vasconi, her oldest son, was already employed as a winemaker, perhaps working under Luigi.)

Gaetano Rossi supervised the building of Lombarda Winery, today's Freemark Abbey. Charles Forni and a host of other Italian and Italian Swiss stonecutters served as his crew.

The third Northern Italian at the Europa, "Captain" Gaetano Rossi, a divorced man, moved around quite a bit. He had been a stonemason back in Italy. He came to Napa County around 1882 and helped run the hotel for a while and then moved to Idaho to do hotel work there. He returned in 1898. As a former stone worker, he understood the architecture involved in building with stone. He would manage the construction of Lombarda Winery. Antonio sent to Italy for an able young man to help them: his nephew Charles Forni, who stepped off the train in San Francisco with $2.75 in his pocket. Antonio met him there, gave him a $25.00 gold piece and escorted him to St. Helena.

Other Italian-speaking families lived close by and became part of Lombarda's building crew. Some of them were related to Antonio Forni or Ted Arrighi, either directly or through marriage. Joe Bognotti, for example, was a stonemason. He and his wife, Teodolinda, rented space in their house to their nephew, Emil Forni, and to laborers John Poggi and Joe Ghiringhelli. An Italian Swiss, Joseph Pedroni, was also a stonemason, as was Francisco

Giugni, who had some strong young sons. Young men from the Gagetta, Pocai, Pelissa and Navone families also participated.

Captain Rossi found a promising site from which to quarry volcanic rocks for the new building near Glass Mountain, not far from the vineyard. The men lifted boulders onto wagons, and teams of horses hauled them to the building site. Under the supervision of Joe Bognotti and Francisco Giugni, Charles Forni and a few others learned to turn round boulders into square, well-fitting building blocks. They installed the blocks around the outside perimeter of Mrs. Tychson's old winery, forming an attractive shell.

Younger siblings hung around the construction site, trying to make themselves useful. The sisters of the workers stopped by often, too, to check on the work, serve refreshments and flirt. Romances developed. Jealousies flared. Many of the men and women who worked on Lombarda eventually planted vineyards, and some started small wineries of their own. They formed a vital new stratum in the population profile of St. Helena, often replacing Anglo-Saxon pioneer families who moved on to other endeavors elsewhere. Young Charles Forni found himself locked in some kind of ongoing battle with Ted Arrighi. Charles left town and accepted a vineyard job in Cloverdale, on land owned by Walter Sink, a St. Helena neighbor. Forni would return to the Napa Valley at a critical time with a new set of skills unrelated to stonemasonry.

Another to migrate from the southern Alpine slopes was Secondo Nichelini, a Swiss, who settled in Sonoma and opened a bakery and pasta business. His brother Francisco joined him there sometime around 1880, soon followed by Francisco's son Anton. It would be Anton Nichelini who would father a winemaking family in the Napa Valley. Anton trained in France as a stonecutter and builder. While working in his uncle's business, he became friends with Henry Chauvet, whose father was a pioneer Sonoma vintner. Henry introduced Anton to another Italian Swiss, Caterina Corda, whom Anton married after a brief romance. Anton and Caterina were eventually able to homestead land in Chiles Valley, in the untamed hills east of St. Helena once owned by pioneer and whiskey maker Joe Chiles. The land, it turned out, had significant deposits of two minerals: magnesite and chromium. Anton developed a small mining company to capitalize on this convenient and valuable resource. He also planted grapes. He erected a temporary winery on the slopes of a hill and used a Roman lever press to crush his own harvest and that of his wine-growing neighbors, weighing their grapes at the mine's scale. With his stonecutting ability, he was able to build a small, expertly crafted winery down slope from the first,

Some of the Lombarda workers gathered with their families for a picnic. Notice Antonio Forni's longing glance (upper right, with glass in hand). *Courtesy of Leslie Crenna.*

Many of these Sons of Italy turned to bootlegging.

Caterina and Anton Nichelini founded a Napa Valley winery that remained in production before, during and after Prohibition. *Courtesy of Dave Patterson.*

which was completed in 1895 and is still in use today by his descendants. He worked hard and without pretense, made good wine (perhaps with Henry Chauvet's help at first) and prospered. He further augmented his bottom line by establishing a mobile culinary service (mainly wine and bread) for his own miners and the workers in other Napa County mines to sustain them during their labors. The manufacture, sale and delivery of wine, all of which would eventually become illegal, helped the Nichelinis develop deep roots and many connections in the Napa Valley despite the remoteness of their location.

Theodore Gier, a German, also became an important figure in the wine industry around the turn of the century. He operated a grocery store and then a small wine and liquor store in Oakland and used the proceeds from that to establish a distillery, Metropole Whiskey. He bought land on Mount Veeder in Napa's western hills, where he built a large winery he called Sequoia. He also bought land on Spring Mountain, west of St. Helena. Like William Scheffler, he continued to buy vineyard land not only on the hillsides but also on the valley floor, including an old (1879) vineyard at the site of today's Hall Winery, just south of St. Helena. He even bought Scheffler's old Edge Hill. He called his combined acreage Giersburg.

Gier had friends in many places, including his native Germany, where Kaiser Wilhelm had honored him for his services in the Boxer Rebellion. His contemporaries in Oakland honored him as well, making him president and director of the Merchants' Exchange. He helped found the Oakland Chamber of Commerce and was a founder and director of Oakland's Security Bank & Trust Company. A contemporary biographer called him "the leader in the wine industry in California" and "a splendid representative of the prominent manufacturer and capitalist to whom business is but one phase of life." He was a colorful, flamboyant character with few compunctions and a strong sense of entitlement. As far as Gier was concerned, the temperance movement posed little danger to him or to the wine industry. In defiance of its complaint that adults' drinking habits adversely affected their children, one of his Metropole Whiskey business cards featured four children with a wagon and a dog. His ebullience may have persuaded others in the Napa Valley that there would soon be a cure for Wayne Wheeler and his pesky ilk, just like there had been a remedy for phylloxera and could be for chronic intemperance, at least according to some.

Just a short walk from the town's center, the Beringer brothers (Jacob and Fritz) had a winery that produced a well-recognized brand of fine wines. They had utilized low-cost labor in the 1870s to construct most of their facilities, including a temperature-constant cave dug into the volcanic rock immediately behind the winery. Beringer was family owned and family run, and the Beringers themselves were friendly, without the pretense that seemed to characterize some of the other winery owners. They were also realistic—more like farmers than European nobility. Their elegantly appointed Rhine House mansion, just north of St. Helena, was a point of pride for the small wine town. They watched the temperance movement with a wary eye.

Less than a mile to the north, on the opposite side of the county road, Charles Krug's nephew, Bismarck Bruck, had taken over the ailing Krug facility and made it modestly profitable. Seen as something of a hero and a potential spokesman for wine interests, he was elected to several public offices, including the state assembly. Known as Pete by his friends and followers, the good-looking Bruck changed his religious affiliation from Catholic to Episcopalian and was a favorite with the Napa Valley's original American pioneer descendants.

In addition to its many wineries, the Napa Valley had a few important breweries to slake the thirsts of the stonecutters and small farmers who were moving in. Replete as it was with Germans, the wine town of St. Helena was also a beer town, with a good *braumeister.*

The Beringer family's Rhine House was a St. Helena landmark. *Courtesy of St. Helena Historical Society.*

Edward Fautz left his hometown of Baden, Germany, and was turning much of the upper valley's eighty-three acres of hops into a very drinkable beer. Fautz, his Swiss wife, Louisa Zimmerman Fautz, and his German assistant, Leopold Wert, practiced their craft at the St. Helena Brewery, located partway up what is now Spring Mountain Road but was then a winding, unpaved cart path known as Brewery Lane, terminating not far from the Beringer winery. Steep in places, the rustic byway may have been a challenge for the horses that drew wagons full of beer kegs and bottles down to his saloon, the St. Helena Brewery Saloon, in town. Customers cheered one another with drinking songs and Germanic wit, like *Alkohol und Nikotin Rafft die halbe Menschheit hin. Aber ohne Schnapps und Rauch Stirbt die andere Hälfte auch.* ("Alcohol and nicotine destroy half of mankind. But without brandy and smoke, the other half will perish, too.")

The brewery and the Fautzes' home were located near the old city reservoir in the western hills. The home was more than a simple residence. How much more is open to conjecture, as random people seem to have spent the night there from time to time. It's not a stretch to imagine that paid female companionship was available there. One who could have testified to

George Blaufuss's brewery was a treasured resource for Napans before Prohibition. Blaufuss tried to operate it during Prohibition, too, but he got caught. *Courtesy of George Blaufuss Jr.*

that was local blacksmith George Kettlewell. Kettlewell had the misfortune of being present at 7:00 a.m. one morning when Fautz's house burned down. The local newspaper reported that Kettlewell was slightly injured by a falling coal. What, one wonders, was Kettlewell doing halfway up Spring Mountain at that time of day?

Fautz replaced the burned structure with a tall, narrow new home that was thirty by forty-two feet with a nine-foot lower story to be used as a brewery and an eleven-foot upper story containing no fewer than nine rooms. It must have resembled a warren. The home/brewery's grand opening on July 4 featured dice games and was very well attended, and had any of the partiers found themselves too inebriated to navigate their way home, they might have resorted to a berth in one of the little chambers upstairs—alone or perhaps with a paid companion. That may explain how the U.S. Census happened to count Swiss wine grower Joseph Baretta and "house maid" Maria Ryhwer (the census probably misspelled both names) at Fautz's place and maybe why Kettlewell happened to be there to receive the falling embers.

In addition to the American brewer/banker Edward Churchill, a popular German *braumeister* also operated in the city of Napa, George Blaufuss. His Napa Brewery on Soscol and Eighth Streets contained large vats of beer. It went in barrels to local saloons like Dave Cavagnaro's Brooklyn Hotel across the First Street Bridge in "Italian Town." Some customers came to the brewery itself to refill their private kegs. Among George's private clientele was Judge Percy King, who would one day have to make a controversial decision about his old friend George.

Chapter 3
POWERFUL FORCES

ASL, WCTU, SDA

While the wine business was trying to recover, the Anti-Saloon League was making considerable progress toward seeing that it didn't. The ASL's head attorney and chief lobbyist, Wayne Wheeler, was getting his message into newspapers and ASL-friendly candidates into public office. His influence had begun in his native Ohio but soon extended to all states, including California. At first his main audience was not the elite who already ran the country but the electorate who supported them and the candidates who longed to unseat them. He continued to work through mainline Protestant churches—Methodist, Presbyterian, Baptist, Lutheran, Episcopal and Congregational—and some newer organizations, like the Seventh Day Adventists, heirs to the Millerite movement of the 1840s; and the Mormons, who for political reasons of their own shied away from the ASL. Wheeler forwarded the WCTU's message by targeting saloons, which were the domain of men. Men ate lunch in saloons, congregated there after work and went there after the meetings of their Masonic groups and other brotherhoods. They spent too much of their paychecks there, especially when they included gambling and prostitutes in their evening entertainment. The presence of these technically outlawed enterprises suggested both police laxity and widespread political corruption. Many an American mayor/judge/police chief had literally been caught with his pants down in saloon-related adventures. Framing it as a movement to improve America's morality, Wheeler presented the debate about alcohol as a contest between the churches and the saloons. Women loved this idea. The goal also began to change. No longer was the endgame about temperance in drink; the complete prohibition of alcoholic products became the desired outcome. Temperance gave way to prohibition.

Wayne Wheeler was crazy smart. "Crazy" in the sense of being mentally ill was a descriptor that fit another beacon in the prohibition movement, Carry Nation. She was a large, imposing, stern-faced woman without much formal education. The Civil War was a disaster for her Kentucky slaveholding family. Carry herself befriended and socialized with the family's black staff and might have gone on to do significant humanitarian work had she not, in 1867, married a chain-smoking alcoholic named Charles Gloyd. Their daughter was born with birth defects, for which Carry blamed Charles. She divorced him and married David Nation, a preacher-cum-lawyer, in Medicine Lodge, Kansas. She eventually became proprietor of a small hotel and, with that success behind her, started a local branch of the WCTU. She adopted some of Mother Eliza Thompson's methods to get her prohibitionist message across; she serenaded saloonkeepers with temperance hymns, sometimes accompanying herself with a hand organ. Voices in her head that she believed came from God then told her to go to the community of Kiowa, Kansas, and throw things. She obeyed and hurled rocks at three saloons, which she destroyed. Her choice of weapons escalated to the use of a hatchet, which she employed against the wares of the local drugstore, a major distributor of alcohol. The hatchet became a permanent part of her repertoire.

Newspaper journalists throughout America became aware of Carry's exploits; reports on her "hatchetations" in the first years of the twentieth century were national news, and Carry became a celebrity. Carry's mother suffered psychotic delusions and was permanently hospitalized; Carry herself probably suffered from a mental disorder of some kind as well (she seemed quite humorless about her antics), but she was actually able to support herself by speaking for a fee, publishing a newsletter and a newspaper (*The Hatchet*) and marketing hatchet-related memorabilia.

The *Napa Daily Journal* ran a story about one of Carry's raids in February 1901: "Mrs. Nation launched her crusade against the joints at an early hour this morning. She arose at 4:30 and soon afterwards started a tour of joint-smashing." On that particular occasion, she happened to nick herself in the forehead with the axe and so was dripping with blood. "[She] turned over two large slot machines and smashed the glass in front of each. She soon made a wreck of a large refrigerator, and after that turned her attention to the liquor and the fixtures behind the bar. A keg of beer then came the way of her hatchet."

Prohibition forces were present in Napa County. A copycat hatcheter appeared in Napa City. He was a young dentist named Charles Farman, who got up early one morning to "carry-nationize" the bar at the Revere House hotel across from the courthouse. He was on the way to the Oberon Bar down the street when he was arrested. Farman was a lifelong foe of alcohol and even ran for office on the Prohibition Party ticket in the 1930s. A WCTU chapter formed in wine-happy St. Helena and, with little or no publicity, had twenty members. The Methodist, Presbyterian and Seventh Day Adventist churches combined for a special, ecumenical WCTU meeting, with prizes for original essays and poetry and entertainment by the choir of the St. Helena Sanitarium (now the St. Helena Hospital). The keynote speaker was a Dr. Abbott, who lectured on the horrors of alcohol. According to the *St. Helena Star* on July 15, 1910, he informed the audience of the latest research confirming that alcohol is "always and only a poison" that "in the minutest doses has an injurious effect on the human system, never promoting, but always destroying health." This was standard pedagogical fare that would have warmed the heart of Mary Hanchett Hunt but had no basis in fact.

The teetotaling Seventh Day Adventist Church had (and still has) a particularly strong presence in Napa County. Ellen G. White, its main prophet, lived near St. Helena, the heart of the wine country. A childhood injury where she was hit in the face by a brick altered her life, and some resulting brain damage may have contributed to her occasional very vivid "visions," trance-like states where she believed she saw and heard messages from God. Unlike the violent anti-saloon instructions Carry Nation experienced, White's visions were reassuring and involved bright lights and a strong feeling of the presence of God. They encouraged her to remain on the spiritual path the Millerites had begun and to encourage others to do so too. At least one vision revealed to her the importance of health reform. This included more than merely avoiding alcohol. Among her ideas, radical for her day but not unlike those of Diocletian Lewis, were exposure to clean air, pure water, sunshine and exercise and a vegetarian diet that was rich in grains. She was solidly in the camp of those who believed rural life to be more salubrious than that of the city.

White was not without animosity toward the wine industry and those who supported it. When the earthquake and resulting fire brought San Francisco to its knees in 1906, she was delighted, believing the end of the world was finally nigh and was beginning, as she had long suspected, in the most reprobate places. She wanted her driver to take her to where she could get a good view of the devastation.

"Sister White," as she was called, would have been pleased to hear that the CWA lost some 10 million gallons of wine in the catastrophe. Also destroyed was a cache of super premium blends it had stored away for special aging, with the intention of introducing to the market a few years later. In Oakville, 100,000 gallons of CWA wine splashed to the ground at Nouveau Medoc, which had been renamed the French-American Wine Company. Charles Carpy's French American Bank in San Francisco turned to ash, and his Napa City winery crumbled.

THEODORE BELL

Ellen White was a well-known national and even international figure. Another St. Helena resident who had made a name for himself was Theodore Bell. Bell's family owned the site in the hills east of town that eventually became Bell Canyon Reservoir, the city's main water supply. When young Theodore was growing up there, it sported forty acres of grapevines. Ted was a highly intelligent child who attended school in a small building less than a mile from his house. After graduation, he returned there to teach, and during recess and after school, he studied law there. He passed the bar exam on his twenty-fifth birthday and in 1898 was made district attorney of Napa County. Shortly before the turn of the century, he helped the sheriff's department stop a highwayman named Buck English by shooting him in the hip.

Bell figured prominently in helping San Franciscans recover from the devastation of 1906. With his assistance, scores of Italians, their North Beach homes and businesses destroyed, found new lives in Napa, adding their numbers to the compatriots who had just preceded them. Their presence created a shift in the political character of the county seat that worked against the mildly prohibitionist trend there.

Bell attracted the attention of San Francisco politician James D. Phelan, a Democrat who had served as mayor from 1897 to 1902. In 1903, with Phelan's backing, Bell ran for state assembly and won, one of only a handful of Democrats to do so in a state congress that was overwhelmingly Republican. His opponent was Frank Coombs, a second-generation Napan

whose father was one of Napa's very first Caucasian pioneers. Bell lost when he ran again in the next assembly election and lost again three more times when he ran for governor. Nevertheless, his party held him in high esteem and sent him to the Democratic National Convention in 1908. He gave the nomination speech for William Jennings Bryan's bid for the presidency and campaigned with Bryan. Bryan was a gifted speaker, a fundamentalist Christian and a prohibitionist— strange company for the wine country's favorite son. (To no avail, however; William Howard Taft defeated Bryan, as William McKinley had done twice before.) Bell went again in 1912, only to see Bryan throw his support to Woodrow Wilson.

Top: Congressman Theodore Arlington Bell would become a major player in the Democratic Party and a powerful advocate for the alcoholic beverage industry. *Courtesy of the California State Library, Sacramento, California.*

Bottom: Bismarck Bruck in 1914. State assemblyman, county supervisor and member of the St. Helena Board of Trustees, pioneer descendant Bismarck Bruck managed the ranch of his uncle, Charles Krug, and when Prohibition came, he made grape juice there. *Courtesy of Kergan Bruck.*

To protect his own political career, Bell needed to make sure he didn't anger either his wine country constituency or his teetotaling mentor. He found a clever way to make himself acceptable to both. He lobbied for legislation to tax wine more heavily. The tax increase would be mild on pure, unadulterated wine but harshly punitive on wines to which sugar had been added, a practice common in Ohio and Missouri, where the grape-growing season was shorter. Naturally, this angered winemakers in Ohio and Missouri and did nothing to promote harmony in the wine industry as a whole, although California vintners were happy. On the surface, Bell's position may have made him appear antagonistic to the wine industry. Bell believed, however, that the more money the government could collect from intoxicants, the less likely it would be to prohibit them. A pure wine act would also guarantee against adulterants like molasses, rum, logwood and lead. Bell's ideas were consonant with the popular and necessary Pure Food Act of 1906, which outlawed the manufacture, sale and transportation of poisonous patent medicines, including those with high alcohol content.

WINE V. BEER V. BOOZE

Influential representatives of the wine industry followed Theodore Bell's lead and tried to convince members of Congress that wine was a "health food." It was consumed in fine restaurants and not in beer halls or saloons and thus did not lead toward moral corruption, like beer and booze did, they argued. Much was made of the California State Board of Health's findings that California wines, especially those of the California Grape Growers' Association, were pure and not adulterated. This would be part of the wine industry's theme for the next ten years.

The other part of their message was that Europeans incorporated wine in their everyday lives without ill effect, so Americans could too, and should. The *San Francisco Call* printed this bit of propaganda in April 1909: "It has been shown by documentary evidence from our American consuls in all great wine producing and grape growing countries where this healthy beverage is universally consumed that intemperance is practically unknown." This was the same mythology that Jefferson had promoted a century earlier. Jefferson considered himself a light drinker and consumed, he said, three to four and a half glasses of wine every night. Perhaps the glasses were small.

Leaders in the beer business also tried to separate themselves from the manufacturers of hard liquor. Like winemakers, they tried to convince the electorate that beer was healthy and good. Beer, the United States Brewers' Association insisted, was "liquid bread," made of wholesome ingredients like barley and hops. Among these leaders were men with surnames like Busch, Pabst and Schlitz. They may not have realized that the very fact that Germans, most of them Catholic, made and drank it was not a selling point in the less tolerant East and Midwest. It would soon become even less so. Saloonkeepers, especially those connected to breweries, combated the prohibitionists' complaints that their businesses were squalid pits of corruption by agreeing to curfews.

Manufacturers of whiskey tried to separate themselves from the saloons. They created a Model License League that lobbied to limit the number of licenses for saloons and to revoke the licenses of those that broke the law by serving to minors. In the short view, this made sense, since the ASL seemed to be targeting the establishments where beer was served. In the long run, however, agreeing with the Drys about anything only worsened the Wets' position. No one seemed to be questioning the underlying concept that drinking alcoholic beverages was immoral or that the federal government had the right to interfere with adults' decisions in these matters. As the twentieth century progressed, Congress's encroachment on the rights of American citizens would reach astonishing proportions, but because it was gradual and apparently sanctioned by boards of education and mainstream churches, few outside the alcoholic beverage industry seemed alarmed.

Many in the Napa Valley continued to be optimistic about the industry's future. Felix Salmina, for example, foresaw good things for his meticulously kept Larkmead winery and the wine industry at large. After a fire destroyed his home, he commissioned a prominent architect to design a fine, expensive new one.

Those who were closer to government and public policy were more pessimistic, however, as they observed the election of more and more Drys into public office. Wine country voters continued to send Bismarck Bruck, Charles Krug's nephew, to the state assembly in Sacramento. Deeply concerned about the future of the wine industry, Bruck tried to go with the nonalcoholic flow by producing and marketing unfermented grape juice. He sold shares in a new venture, the Bruck Grape Juice Company, for ten dollars each. He packaged the product in pint- and quart-sized bottles and offered juice from both red and white grapes. He touted his wares as "absolutely non-alcoholic...Not only a delightful beverage, but...absolutely pure, and

Vintner and state assemblyman Bismarck Bruck formed a grape juice company.

unlike most temperance drinks, a health-giving tonic." One morning, when things were looking especially grim for the wine industry, Bruck distributed small bottles of his juice brew to each of his fellow members of the California Assembly. It was a good idea, but the grapes that made good wine did not make an especially appealing soft drink. Manufacturers like Welch's in the East, where tangy, juicy Concord grapes thrived in the colder climate, had the advantage. (Thomas Welch and his son Charles were ardent prohibitionists from northern New York State who, like the hatchetizing Napan Charles Farman, were also dentists. Thomas developed a method of pasteurizing grape juice that kept it from fermenting.) The CWA also marketed grape juice, using fruit from the Central Valley and Southern California. It, too, heard the distant drumbeats and was researching ways to survive, but its grape juice was also bland and would never bring it the kind of revenue it was used to making from the sale of premium wines.

Hoping to give visual evidence that the rural (and therefore healthy) wine country produced a pure, life-enhancing product, the city of St. Helena put on a highly publicized Vintage Festival in 1912. The festival showcased the wines of its finest vintners, as well as Bruck's grape juice. There was a parade with floats; there were contests of skill and strength, poetry readings, live music and a play put on by the local high school students; and it concluded with the crowning of a queen. A movie was made of the 1912 festivities. It was one of the first propaganda films ever made, produced with the hope of demonstrating that wine was associated with wholesome fun. People from all over the Bay Area came to the 1912 Vintage Festival, and it was an unqualified success, but in terms of its ability to turn the tide on the prohibition movement, it was but a drop in the bucket.

To further purify the wine country's reputation, Napa County leaders decided to crack down on saloons. There were plenty of them, and some were considered "houses of ill fame," where prostitutes were available. When the City of Napa granted liquor licenses to three more such places in 1909, many people were angry—not about the brothels in the back of the house but about the liquor. The editor of the *Weekly Calistogan* wrote an editorial about it on New Year's Day 1909. "Men may differ as to the necessity of the so-called social evil," he said, "but there can be no defensible excuse for permitting liquor to be dispensed at such places."

St. Helena was home to several busy brothels over the years, but the most famous was the Stone Bridge Saloon. It was located across the road from what is today the Pope Street Bridge, which spans the Napa River and provides an entrance to St. Helena from the east. It was the successor to several other bridges that had been washed away by winter storms. The ford that preceded the bridges was once called the Whiskey Crossing. It got that name when an employee of Joe Chiles stole a case or so of his employer's liquor and cached it there in the 1870s, suggesting that a house of ill fame may have operated there even then. (Otherwise why would he have stashed it at that particular location?) It was also there that the body of August Rosenbaum was found in 1889.

A Russian woman named Mary Selowski ran the place. She had a stable of girls who came from as far away as the southern states to provide their own brand of comfort and consolation to generations of men. They also provided alcohol. Mary was fined $250 for some infraction—perhaps violating the midnight curfew—and the place was temporarily shut down. After it reopened, Peter Cesari shot Dominic Decarlo at the Stone Bridge over a disagreement in a card game, but the brothel continued to operate. Its patrons—some of them reputed to be in law enforcement—appreciated the Stone Bridge, but it was a terrible life for the women, at least one of whom

The Stonebridge Saloon across from the Pope Street Bridge in St. Helena was a house of ill repute. *Courtesy of the St. Helena Historical Society.*

was tricked into working there by her unsavory family. She cried profusely every day. Finally, Mary paid a young man to drive her back to her home in the Southeast, a trip that took weeks.

Some Napa Valley saloons really were quite disreputable. In 1910, the City of St. Helena voted to briefly suspend the licenses of three bars that had stayed open after midnight. The saloon run by W.C. Grimes, a recent arrival from Kern County, was declared a "disgrace" and closed permanently. Whatever went on there included more than the simple sipping of beer. Jules Maggetti's bar across from the depot in Oakville also won the epithet "disgraceful." Maggetti's establishment made the papers several times as the scene of bar fights.

BLIND PIGS IN YOUNTVILLE

There was a particularly heavy concentration of saloons in the little town of Yountville. When the Groezingers' Yountville winery went up for sale, one of the first to buy a part of it was Mary Ghirardi, a Swiss who had only recently arrived in America with her husband, Antone, an Italian. The price was right: $10 for a small parcel of land on Madison Street, the main drag. They also purchased some hilly property just west of Yountville, where Antone ran a small dairy farm. This piece they bought from "Bud" Whitton, the son of pioneer grape grower Green Whitton, whose vines had taken a hit from phylloxera. Bud already owned a Yountville saloon and bought another small parcel in town around the same time Mary did. Mary saw to the construction of a saloon, which she managed starting in 1902. It was successful, so she bought a second Groezinger parcel for $280 and then a third for $400. The rise in price for these small tracts of commercial property reflected an improvement in the value of the land on Madison as the town began to congeal around these watering holes. Within a short time, she had acquired six pieces of what had once been the Groezingers' domain and was probably the community's main commercial landowner.

Now the landlord of several saloons, Mary Ghirardi could supply alcohol to the growing population of vets ensconced at the California Veterans Home a short distance west of the town. The population at the Veterans Home had reached one thousand by the turn of the century—one thousand thirsty, aged, impecunious single men (mostly) with little else to do except regale each other with war stories, well lubricated with liquor. A review of the 1900 U.S. Census reveals that although the non-veteran population of Yountville was only about seven hundred, counting children, there appear to have been at least seven saloons, four of them run by Europeans. In contrast, there was one butcher, one druggist, one cobbler, one liveryman, two blacksmiths, two grocers, two hotels and a couple of launderers, some of them in Yountville and the rest in the whistle stop up the road, Oakville. There were also several "dressmakers." "Dressmaker" was sometimes a euphemism for madam.

The vets had very little money to spend, so Mary needed a gimmick of some sort to trim her overhead and maximize profits. Some of her fellow barkeeps offered ladies for the vets' pleasure, but this does not appear to have been so in Mary's case, as she raised six children in town and would hardly have had the space for such an operation. Antone let a seventh child—a young niece— live with him and the cows up in the hills, a scene reminiscent of the novel *Heidi*. The niece may have earned her keep by helping him with the cows and churning butter, the mainstay of their dairy operation. In addition to the cows and their niece, the Ghirardis had, on their property in the western hills, a large still, where they could brew an inventory of moonshine for a fraction of the wholesale cost and without the requisite taxes. There was plenty of water for it, because the pipes that Groezinger used to run water from his reservoirs down to his winery passed right by the Ghirardis' place and could easily be diverted. Who actually built the ramshackle edifice that housed the still is unclear, but it does not appear to have been Antone. The structures he put on the property display better craftsmanship. It could have been Bud Whitton, who owned the property before the Ghirardis, or even Billy Baldridge and Joe Chiles. Two full-time employees helped with the operation: husband and wife, both chronic inebriates, who lived somewhere on the Ghirardi property, perhaps on the top floor of the structure that housed the still. Antone abetted his wife by trading homemade butter for sugar, mash and other ingredients for home-brewed whiskey.

Attuned to the spirit of the times, there were those who were scandalized about the presence of so much alcoholic temptation so close to such a large contingent of American war heroes. The vets themselves, of course, were just fine with it, but in 1908, an ordinance was passed closing all alcohol-serving establishments within a 1.5-mile radius of the Veterans Home. The saloonkeepers of Yountville were doomed, but before they would admit defeat, some of them tried to sell their wares on the sly. They operated "blind pigs," where individuals wanting to buy booze used a code word, like, "I came to see your blind pig," in order to gain entry to the back room where the liquor was sold. Such enterprises were also called speakeasies, especially when entertainment was also available. The county of Napa hired a man named Hardin to snoop about town and bust the blind pigs of Yountville. He found several. Unfortunately for Mary Ghirardi, one was hers. She was arrested in the summer of 1909 and given the choice of paying a $500 fine (twice what the Stone Bridge's Mary Selowski was charged) or spending one hundred days in the county jail. She chose jail. After a few days there, she changed her mind and petitioned the governor to have her sentence commuted because of her advanced age of fifty-seven. The governor returned the case to the county, and it was ruled that she could be released if she paid the fine. She did and suffered severe poverty ever after; the butter business was not nearly so lucrative as the booze business had been.

The long arm of the law appears to have spared Bud Whitton, who may or may not have stayed in business after 1908. He developed other problems, however. After a sickness lasting several months and therefore ostensibly giving him enough time to get his affairs in order, he died intestate in 1914, leaving a wife and three children in poverty. For the scion of an important pioneer family, his obituary was surprisingly brief, giving rise to the speculation that he succumbed to an occupational hazard and died of drink.

Examining who was penalized, how much and what for suggests that before Prohibition actually became the law, Napa County's attempts to clean up the wine country were laced with small-town cronyism. Peter Guillaume, for example, owned and operated a popular saloon in Yountville. When he was arrested in 1914, he hired a defense attorney, Theodore Bell's brother Edward. Guillaume was able to beat the rap. Shortly after he reopened, patrons had to duck when the extremely intoxicated Edward Fortier staggered about with a knife in a jealous rage over his wife and another man.

Another Yountville saloonkeeper was arrested after the Guillaume incident: Madge Righly. (This might not have been her real name. No Righly is listed in the U.S. Census, and the *Napa Journal* often protected citizens by disguising their names.) Edward Bell defended her too, and during the trial an actual fistfight broke out between Bell and the frustrated district attorney, Nathan Coombs. Nathan was the son of Frank Coombs, the man Edward's brother Theodore had defeated for a seat in the state assembly back in 1904. Edward left Napa and opened a law office in Oakland, but he maintained an active interest in Napa County, especially its darker side.

Chapter 4

THE NOOSE TIGHTENS

Amending the Constitution

Taxes on alcohol had been providing a good portion of the federal government's operating costs ever since the Whiskey Rebellion. They helped finance the Spanish-American War of 1898, which was still fresh in people's minds fifteen years later. The Treasury Department drew from a second source as well during war years: the general public. A flat tax of 3 percent on annual incomes over $800 helped fund the Civil War, and when that proved insufficient, Congress levied a graduated tax of 3 to 5 percent on incomes exceeding $600. The income tax went away in 1866.

Prohibiting booze, wine and beer altogether would bar access to an important tax resource and would endanger the nation's ability to put boots on the ground. Drys believed that creating a permanent tax on incomes would fix this problem. Theodore Bell's mentor William Jennings Bryan, who was serving as secretary of state, vigorously supported the notion of an income tax. Concerned that too few people had accumulated too much wealth and hence too much political influence, many members of Congress joined the Populist Bryan in trying to bring back the tax on personal income.

Passage of a personal income tax would greatly satisfy Wayne Wheeler. It had the potential to diminish the war chests of elite candidates, making it easier for his own handpicked nominees to be elected. It also would smooth the way for his ultimate goal—the prohibition of intoxicants—by replacing their tax-generating power with what he believed were the endlessly deep pockets of the rich. Wealthy industrialists in the Northeast didn't like the idea at all, and for this reason southerners, still angry about the Civil War and its Reconstruction aftermath, liked it a lot. With few Catholics and fewer Jews, most of the heavily Baptist Southland stalwartly supported the prohibition movement and the personal income tax.

The main exception to this was the old French settlement of New Orleans, which continued as an important and profitable market for Napa Valley wines and other alcoholic beverages. Oakville's French-American Winery (formerly Brun and Chaix's Nouveau Medoc) was now in the hands of the California Wine Association. It sold very well to the Francophiles in New Orleans. De Latour's Beaulieu wines were also a favorite there. Napa Valley wines were popular in other big cities and their surrounding suburbs as well, where they continued to be marketed as the preferred beverage of the well-to-do, but this theme did not play well with the average consumer.

With the full force of the Anti-Saloon League, the Populists/Progressives and the South behind it, the U.S. Congress passed the Sixteenth Amendment to the Constitution in 1913. It stated, "Congress shall have power to lay and collect taxes on incomes, from whatever source derived, without apportionment among the several states, and without regard to any census or enumeration."

The Seventeenth Amendment followed close behind the Sixteenth, also in 1913, and it also played into Wayne Wheeler's hand. This one had to do with election reform. Previously, United States senators had been elected by their state legislatures without much involvement from the general public. Successful businessmen like George Hearst, for example, father of publisher William Randolph Hearst and twice senator from California, were thus able to secure their influence by networking nationally. This new amendment called for direct elections of senators by the people for terms of six years. For Wheeler, this was a way to harvest influence in the highest levels of government, because it was the grass-roots electorate—everyday people—whom the prohibitionists were wooing. The entrenched elite who had provided so many senators in the past found themselves being shouldered out of the political arenas that had been their domain since the earliest days of the Republic.

Theodore Bell knew that mopping up local saloons and slapping fines on old ladies in Yountville would do nothing to stop the freight train that was bearing down on the wine industry. Bell had been the Democratic candidate for governor of California in 1906 and 1910 and came fairly close to winning both times. He decided to sit out the 1914 election, but he went on tour throughout the state and spoke directly to Californians about the danger to the state economy and the quality of their own lives if prohibition became the law. Taking a page from Wheeler's book, he urged his audiences not to elect into office anyone who was Dry. He named names, and he spoke about the cozy union between the ASL and recently elected politicians. He also warned his audiences about a petition that was being circulated around the country to ban alcohol altogether. In December 1914, a representative from Alabama brandished that petition—150 feet long with more than six million signatures—while introducing legislation to outlaw the manufacture and sale of alcohol. A majority voted for it in Congress, but passage would have required the consent of two-thirds. It fell just short.

Napa Valley wine interests conceptualized prohibition as a movement that could be thwarted at the state level and tweaked at the federal with compromises regarding taxation that would benefit Californians. The tax on sweetened wine that Bell had forwarded, however, was having unintended consequences. Angry midwestern vintners managed to get Congress to tax brandy, a commodity nearly all of the Napa winemakers produced. West Coast lobbyists sped to Washington to negotiate a compromise that rescinded the tax on sugar in return for eliminating the tax on brandy. They also believed that positive public relations were still possible. The "purity" issue was part of this, as was a general distancing from both beer (saloons) and hard liquor, which were seen as pleasures of the lower classes, while wine continued to be marketed as a beverage enjoyed by the cultured in their chateaux.

PUBLIC RELATIONS

The concept of public relations was on the cutting-edge in the years just before Prohibition became law. The opening of the Panama Canal in 1914 provided the opportunity to create much goodwill for California, which could now send its products to the East Coast by ship instead of the much costlier railroad. To celebrate this iconic achievement, San Francisco planned to host a Panama-Pacific Exposition in 1915 that honored the people and products of the Golden State. This included the wine industry. The California Viticultural Committee would have its own pavilion, a display that would prove to the world that its wine country was on par with that of France and Germany. Wine experts from around the world were invited. The exposition would dignify the industry and help distinguish it from the less noble products of hops and mash. The film of St. Helena's

The Napa Valley had displays at the Panama-Pacific Exposition and ran a propaganda film about wholesome life in the wine country. Shown here is Bismarck Bruck's grape juice, politically correct for its time. *Courtesy of Kergan Bruck.*

1912 Vintage Festival was aired there and proved to be a popular attraction. Rutherford's Inglenook Winery walked away with twenty-one of twenty-three possible awards for premium wines.

Few of the great European vintners could come to taste Inglenook's delicious wines, however, because of another story that dominated the headlines: Europe had gone to war. U-boats prowled the Atlantic; the French and Germans, whom the wine industry had extolled as paragons of culture, were now killing each other. With the sinking of the *Lusitania* and other acts of aggression, American sentiment toward the Germans, already negative because of their saloons and their Catholicism, got worse. Allusions to the elegant nobility and their castled estates of Europe, once at the heart of the Napa Valley's marketing strategy, no longer resonated, especially when the wine was made by families with Teutonic names like Beringer, Gier, Krug and Bruck. Far from drawing new customers to the allure of fine wine, the alcoholic beverage industry's association with people of German descent nudged public opinion further in the opposite direction.

Using the same techniques the ASL had perfected, the federal government's relentless propaganda program fanned the flames of patriotism at the expense of Germany and Germans. Germans now found themselves the objects of dangerous new levels of derision and contempt. German nationals were required to register as "alien enemies." Teachers who had emigrated from Teutonic countries lost their positions, and German language was dropped from curricula. The California superintendent of education ruled that it was permissible for teachers and students to tear out any pro-German references from state-issued textbooks.

The California wine industry completely misread the anti-German sentiment that was gripping the rest of the country. The California Grape Protective Association (CGPA), one of several coalitions that growers formed in the increasingly desperate attempt to save themselves, published this astonishing statement in the *Star* on January 19, 1917:

> *The Association is not wedded to the American saloon. It never has been. It believes the evils of the present system would be practically exterminated if the people would awaken from their provincialism and follow the example of continental Europe. In the cafes and gardens of Germany, France, Italy, Spain, etc., where men and women, priest and rabbi and minister congregate…drunkenness is unknown…and even occasional intoxication is extremely uncommon.*

The CGPA's rhetoric could not have been more ill chosen.

OPTIMISTS AND PESSIMISTS

The Napa Valley's newspapers had always been great boosters of the communities they served. It was becoming increasingly difficult to find positive things to write about. In the summer of 1916, the Republican-leaning *St. Helena Star* took some solace from the fact that San Francisco Democrat James Phelan, then a U.S. senator, was debating Ohio Republican senator Atlee Pomerene about taxes on alcoholic beverages and other items. Congress settled on an added four cents per gallon on dry wine and ten cents per gallon on sweet wine and brandy. There might be a bright side to the increased tax, mused *Star* editor Frank Mackinder. If the United States decided to enter the war in Europe, perhaps the legislators would see how beneficial the alcohol tax was and would shy away from outlawing spirits altogether. Soon additional taxes were added, especially on brandy, whose price per gallon eventually bore an additional fifty-five cents. The price of spirits was now interfering with sales, and who knew what would happen next? Yet another wine delegation went to Washington to remove these burdens, but they were rebuffed. The taxes stayed.

Senator Morris Sheppard, a Texas Democrat, was responsible for killing sales of intoxicating beverages in one very important market. Wine country readers were astonished to learn, one day in 1916, that Congress had passed Sheppard's Bone Dry Act outlawing alcoholic beverages in Washington, D.C., where diplomats from around the world met and discussed matters of state while sipping premium wines from the Napa Valley.

Fearful for its future, the CWA felt the need to shepherd its resources. It only paid local growers a fraction of the contracted price for their grapes. This drove more Napa Valley vineyard owners to sell their acreage. Among the more important properties to turn over was that of John Benson, the San Francisco real estate magnate, who had died in 1910 and left Far Niente to a niece. Industrialist David Perry Doak bought the estate in 1917 and retired there with his new wife, a noted equestrienne named Frieda De Haven, and her daughter Elizabeth. He grew cherries and other fruits at Far Niente, as well as grapes, and he made wine in small quantities. He built a magnificent home and hired John McLaren to landscape it, McLaren having recently laid out Golden Gate Park in San Francisco. McLaren transplanted shrubs, trees and statuary from the Pan-Pacific Exposition.

Doak was another who seemed to minimize the threat of prohibition and apparently felt entitled to do pretty much anything he pleased. His was a classic American success story. He left his family's Missouri farm as

The mansion of Oakville resident David Perry Doak saw opulence and scandal. *Courtesy of the Napa County Historical Society.*

a young man to find his fortune in the banking and investment business and succeeded beyond his wildest dreams after joining forces with railroad magnate Jay Gould. He had irons in many fires, including a quicksilver mine called the New Burlington in Oakville, but his main business interest was the very lucrative Pacific Coast Steel Company, the first modern steel plant on the West Coast. While his wife, Jessie, was living the good life at their home in Los Angeles, his horse-loving girlfriend Frieda was doing the same at Doak's ranch in Oregon. When Jessie discovered the affair, she sued for divorce, and some of the details made it into the *Los Angeles Times.* Several members of his family of origin had already provided a scandal for its readers' pleasure. One of Doak's brothers shot and killed another, and in court their mother, Sarah, sided with the murderer, testifying that the killing was to prevent the victim from taking his three-year-old daughter to Mexico, where she would surely end up leading life of dissolution, or so Sarah testified. The murderer spent the next several decades in prison and in mental institutions while Sarah made a nuisance of herself by hectoring the Oakville Doak for money.

Doak's neighbors, the Churchills, were undergoing family problems as well. Accounts of their internecine lawsuits became juicy reading for the gossip hungry, and their Goodman Bank had to shut its doors. Young

71

Edward Churchill turned his attention to running To Kalon and hoped to save the family fortune.

THE GREAT WAR

Meanwhile, the country was gearing up for war. Saloons continued to be under siege. At the end of 1916, an anti-saloon ordinance came into effect that required all bars to pay seventy-five dollars a month for the right to stay open. Germanophobia also got worse, and in April 1917, just as the United States declared war on Germany, most of the staff at the German consulate in San Francisco were charged with espionage and sabotage in connection with an alleged spy system and a plot to blow up bridges and munitions plants and create havoc in labor unions. Franz Bopp, the consul, was said to have been instrumental in these plans. Bopp came to St. Helena for one last outing with friends before his arrest and subsequent imprisonment. It was a decision that illustrated the mutual admiration that existed between the wine country and Germany. A friend of Bopp's, Frederick Hess, a Swiss German, owned La Jota winery in Angwin and published a German-language newspaper, *California Demokrat*. Hess may have joined Bopp at the inn that night, along with Theodore Gier and other German-speaking St. Helenans. Wisely, Hess decided to shut down the paper as well as the winery. Bopp turned himself in the next day.

Between April 1917 and November 1918, the Dry-friendly U.S. Congress passed several war measures that were intended to remain in effect as long as the country was at war. Many of these laws targeted alcohol in one way or another. A clause in the Selective Service Act of May 1917, which authorized the federal government to raise an army through conscription, stipulated that no alcohol could be served within a five-mile radius of any military installation and no alcohol of any kind could be sold to military personnel. Yountville's economy had already been pulverized by the 1.5-mile restriction in 1908. Another small opportunity took root there, however: the taxi business. Anybody with an automobile could convey thirsty vets to Napa, Rutherford, Oakville or the ever-popular Stone Bridge Saloon in St. Helena.

Now the much larger city of Vallejo was in trouble. Vallejo, adjacent to Napa in Solano County, had a short business street with no fewer than twenty-five saloons. A few years earlier, some navy officials had been so appalled by the city's scurrilous offerings that they threatened to place the naval facility elsewhere, but the assistant secretary of the navy, Franklin Delano Roosevelt, visited Vallejo in 1914 and apparently approved the setting. The closure of the saloons in 1917 resulted in the creation of a new population center in Napa County: Napa Junction, which was five miles from Mare Island. The Portland Cement Company had a plant there, and it was a convergence point for two railroad lines, one running from Sacramento to the Bay Area and the other from Vallejo to Calistoga. It already had a small population of Greeks and Italians. Four saloons cropped up there practically overnight and had a large clientele right away. One of them reported selling 250 cases of hard liquor in a single day. News of brawls and other forms of alcohol-inspired mayhem in Napa Junction became staples in the Napa newspapers, and this nexus that could have become a convenient population center failed to develop much in the first part of the twentieth century.

The Lever Food and Fuel Control Act of 1917, named for the South Carolina Democrat who sponsored it, empowered the president and a new government official, the "food administrator," to authorize what foods could be rationed and/or forbidden because of the war effort. It included language that outlawed the use of certain agricultural products in the manufacture of alcoholic products. The new food administrator was a California Republican named Herbert Hoover. The appearance of "Victory Gardens" and days of the week without sweets, for example, linked the idea of dietary changes with patriotism. Wheat and sugar were rationed, and the amount of alcohol permissible in beer was set at 2.75 percent. This percentage would decrease over the next few months.

On June 25, 1917, ten million American men registered for the draft. Each man was given a number and waited for boot camp to start. A state law in August 1917 put a limit on the number of bars (the word "saloon" was already starting to pass from usage) permitted in any given vicinity. The city of Napa had to reduce from twenty-three to twelve, and those that remained were required to pay the others a closing subsidy. The survivors were: Jules Thebaut, "Buffet," Brown Street; C.L. & J. Carbone, "The Gem," Pearl Street; Franco & Delucca, "The Gilt Edge," Main Street; Nussberger & Mayfield, "The Assembly," Main Street; Roney & Vieusseux, Brown Street; E.H. Manchester, "Oberon," Main Street; Green & Gstrein, Russ House Bar, Brown Street; Charles F. Hargrave, Main Street; A. Zeller, Palace Hotel Bar, Third Street; S.L. Martinelli, Owl Hotel Bar, Main Street; Dave Cavagnaro, Brooklyn Hotel Bar, Third Street; and A. Dollman, Napa Hotel Bar, Main Street. The closing subsidy was a tease because it was becoming clear that it would only buy the "survivors" a few months at best.

In Washington, D.C., the ASL and an army of prohibitionists continued their campaign to make intoxicating substances illegal. As always, their ranks were swelled with women, whose fate as voters was as firmly tied to temperance issues as it had been in the days of Frances Willard and Susan B. Anthony. Just before the state's saloon-closure decree, the U.S. Senate had passed a resolution with most of the wording that would become the Eighteenth Amendment to the Constitution. Texas senator Morris Sheppard, who crafted the bill that turned D.C. Dry, wrote the bulk of it. It would outlaw the manufacture, transportation and sale of alcohol, but it would not penalize citizens for buying and drinking it. It now went to the House of Representatives to be reviewed, fine tuned and voted on, a process that consumed most of the rest of 1917.

More restrictions hit the liquor business. In the summer of 1917, twenty-five states passed laws forbidding whiskey makers from mailing advertisements for distilled beverages. A new federal law prohibited the importation or manufacture of whiskey, but brandy could be used to fortify wines. In reporting about this turn of events on July 24, 1917, the *St. Helena Star* added that President Wilson could cancel permits to make wine or beer at any time, as a war measure.

Wine professionals continued to be divided on how to defend the industry from the now-catastrophic assault. The California Grape Protective Association, whose membership included growers in the Central Valley as well as Southern California, continued to blame hard liquor manufacturers and saloons for corrupting America's morals. It felt that light wines and beers should be exempted from what was surely going to be a national prohibition of some kind. To that end, it supported a piece of legislation called the Rominger Bill that sought to outlaw saloons and the manufacture and importation of whiskey, gin and brandy and the manufacture of wine with more than 14 percent alcohol.

Many Napa County growers began to suspect that supporting proscriptions of any kind played into the movement's hand. Rominger was wrong in principle, they believed. Too late, they realized that the federal government actually had no business involving itself in this matter, especially (they said in an open letter to the CGPA) with a war going on. The defiantly German Theodore Gier was especially outraged. One of his flagship products was Metropole Whiskey. He and others, among them Bismarck Bruck, angrily withdrew from CGPA and denounced the Rominger Bill.

1917 Festivals

Wine was still allowed in September 1917, when St. Helena put on its annual Vintage Festival with the theme "Back to the Soil." Thousands came, many by train and the rest by car, which was no small feat, since the county road was still unpaved. Temporarily out-of-service flivvers lined the side of the road while their owners changed flat tires. The organizers hoped to keep as much "vintage" in the festival as possible. The Inglenook booth proudly displayed its Pan-Pacific awards. Napa's Migliavacca Winery was amply represented. Wine from Beaulieu was plentiful. De Latour had made 160,000 gallons that year. Small-volume vintners like Giuseppi Brovelli's St. Helena Winery also poured their wares. (Brovelli won first place for best advertising display.) Other intoxicants made their appearance at the 1917 Vintage Festival, especially "jackass brandy," alcohol made with grape juice and sugar—the latter suddenly hard to get—that took little time to make and didn't require the time and cool storage space that actual wine did. Rivers of this would soon be streaming from illegal businesses throughout the Napa Valley and many other rural places in California.

On the whole, less wine was available than in previous festivals, and fewer St. Helenans attended. This was partly because many vintners had simply

Leading vintner John Wheeler pulled out most of his vines and planted other crops. *Courtesy of Sandra Learned Perry.*

A Fourth of July parade in St. Helena brought lots of onlookers. The Hotel St. Helena, once home to a saloon, now served ice cream sodas. Bootleggers sold moonshine, which was easy to find. *Courtesy of Sandra Learned Perry.*

given up. Influential industry leader John Wheeler (no relation to Wayne) pulled out most of his eighty-acre vineyard on Zinfandel Lane in St. Helena. He planted prunes and walnuts, and after consulting with industry expert G.C. Husmann, he grafted currants on the remaining grapevines. A well-to-do farmer named W.H. Canavan sold his place on Pope Street, which included a wine cellar and other buildings, to Giuseppi Signorelli, who had been leasing Edge Hill from Theodore Gier. The Canavan/ Signorelli barn still stands at an S in the road just across from Allison Avenue. Even one of the town's doctors left. H.M. Pond, MD, abandoned his offices in Napa and St. Helena and moved to Alameda County.

In contrast, a couple of weeks later, St. Helenans eagerly attended the annual state fair in Napa, which had little to do with alcohol or the presence of tipsy tourists and thus seemed more "patriotic" and "moral," especially for families with children. The parade that marched its way through Napa City featured livestock as well as bands, Masons, floats and the usual constituents of adults and children in uniform. Napa was much less dependent on the wine industry than was its sister city up valley. Given the stress centered on the future of grapes and their fermented presentation, it may have been a relief to ride merry-go-rounds and vote for the best apple pie.

With its tax base shrinking, the city of St. Helena felt the effects of prohibition several years before the Eighteenth Amendment actually became law. It was unable to light the town's streets at night for a time in June 1917 because it couldn't pay its electrical bill. The road service that sprinkled the still unpaved streets with water to keep the dust down was discontinued in July of the following year.

RATIFICATION

Throughout the summer and fall, meanwhile, the Eighteenth Amendment was lumbering its way through the House of Representatives, which made a few changes and, on December 17, 1917, passed it. It would become law if and when three-quarters of the states' legislatures—thirty-six of the then forty-eight states—ratified it. They would have seven years to do so. The editor of the *St. Helena Star* tried to be positive about the city's main industry. He tallied twenty-seven Dry states and nineteen Wet ones. The Wets needed nine from a pool that consisted of California, Connecticut, Delaware, Florida, Illinois, Kentucky, Louisiana, Massachusetts, Minnesota, Nevada, New Jersey, New York, Ohio, Pennsylvania, Rhode Island, Texas, Vermont, Wisconsin and Wyoming. Only nine. Surely there would be nine.

The ratification process commenced just after the start of 1918. Of the first five states to vote for the amendment—Mississippi, Virginia, Kentucky, North Dakota and South Carolina—only Kentucky, with its venerable bourbon industry, could be considered a potential Wet state. The ASL had done a good job of packing Kentucky's state legislature with Drys, as it had done nearly everywhere else in the country. When the birth state of Carry Nation fell on January 14, Wet forces were unhappy. But when the much more cosmopolitan Maryland voted Dry a month later, the writing on the wall was clear to all. It would be another year before the bill made its way through all forty-eight states, but a triumph for the Drys seemed assured.

The California Wine Association read the message, did the math and compared the results to its bottom line. The market for alcoholic beverages was doomed, and even if a miracle occurred and nine states did ratify the amendment, the market for wine would have shrunk too small; continuing to operate at the CWA's present level was not worth it. It had been divesting its properties for some time, but now it pulled out the stops: "The future of the industry is too dark to warrant a continuance of the business," it said in February 1918. It liquidated the rest of its properties.

Sheriff Ed Kelton and his men yearned to make a statement about their position on Prohibition. They had been observing the comings and goings at several questionable sites for weeks. Business boomed at Mary Selowski's Stone Bridge Saloon, which was benefiting from the livery service originating in Yountville, as well as from taxis out of Oakville and Rutherford. Mary and her girls had been operating without much difficulty, but she was finally arrested for liquor violations in November 1918, charged $1,000 and sentenced to six months in jail. In February 1919, Kelton's men swooped in at the Hotel Cecille, a rooming house on Main Street in Napa, and scooped up six offenders, among them an eighteen-year-old waitress and a marine who had shed his uniform and donned civilian apparel so he could get a drink. They also nabbed a sixty-year-old bricklayer, a sixty-five-year-old carpenter, a well-known taxi driver and a porter at the Cecille. They released the porter, remanded the marine to Mare Island and sent the minor to juvenile court. District Attorney Nathan Coombs vowed to prosecute the remaining offenders to the limit. They paid expensive fines and went to jail.

HYSTERIA

In addition to being subjected to increased scrutiny for alcohol violations, citizens were told to be on the lookout for German spies. The St. Helena Police Department arrested a German man who made a derogatory comment about the American flag. Another received a call that he would be tarred and feathered. He fled. An Austrian in Pope Valley, perhaps also the recipient of a hate-filled phone call, shot himself. The Napa police arrested several who were said to be pro-German, but the most frightening episode occurred in Calistoga. One night in March 1918, just a few weeks after the Cecille arrests, Sheriff Kelton led a convoy of sixteen cars up the highway and burst upon a party of six Calistogans who were reported to be celebrating the Kaiser's victories in France. They pushed the terrified men around and forced them to kiss the American flag. A week later, Napa's lead judge, Henry Gesford, declared that seditious people shouldn't be forced to kiss the flag; they should be shot. Not long afterward, one of the best-known men in Calistoga, Felix Grauss, a German Jew, was removed from the post office where he had served for sixteen years as U.S. postmaster and assistant postmaster. He was heard to grumble something negative about the federal government, and the U.S. Secret Service sent a spy of its own to monitor him. The agent also heard him make unhappy utterances, and in September 1918, he was arrested for sedition.

Shortly afterward, the flamboyant and very Germanic Theodore Gier and several of his employees in Oakland were accused of singing German songs and toasting the Kaiser. They were all arrested and, like the Calistogans, made to kiss the American flag. Gier denied the charges and made bail for his crew.

Pro-wine politician Theodore Bell also got caught up in the paranoia. A mob in Berkeley burned down a place of worship belonging to a group of conscientious objectors, the Church of the Living God. Somehow a letter survived the inferno. (Clearly it was planted there to be discovered.) It was from Bell to Reverend Joshua Sykes, agreeing to represent them for $1,000. The California Bar Association accused Bell of "unethical and unpatriotic conduct" and threatened to have him disbarred for extending legal assistance to those who refused to enter active duty. To some, Bell's championing of the wine industry, with all its Germans, imparted a whiff of indecency; his support of conscientious objectors was over the top.

Others in the valley, however, especially those of German ancestry, saw the hysteria for what it was. When Kelton ran for sheriff again in August 1918, he was defeated. The new sheriff was Joe Harris, who would be a major player in much of the drama to come. Harris grew up with wine and had excellent references. His father, James Reed Harris, was the first to plant grapes in the Atlas Peak area of Napa; his wife, Mary, was the sister of prominent Napa lawyer Percy King, who would also figure prominently in the lives of many people in the years to come.

Meanwhile, men from everywhere poured into Europe to participate in the Great War, which by 1918 had become a bloody stalemate, much of it in the once proud vineyards of France. Accompanying them was a microbial monster, a virus people were calling the "Spanish Lady" that mutated into the supervirus we know today as H1N1. Influenza usually began with a nosebleed that was followed quickly by fever and a cough. Pneumonia often developed and then death. The great influenza episode of 1917 and 1918 sped across the globe, taking millions of lives, including quite a few in the party-loving Napa Valley. To stem the contagion, people wore gauze masks and learned to avoid places where groups congregated. They also prayed a lot. Quite naturally, those who believed this horrific episode was an act of God fell to their knees and made bargains to mend their ways. Just about everyone had heard the ASL's message that alcohol was a poison and drinking it was immoral and contrary to the war effort. In a time of escalating terror, alcohol of any kind truly looked like a brew of the devil. Patriotism, prayer and prohibition had become intertwined. They braided together to form a noose that lynched whatever was left of the alcoholic beverage industry.

Chapter 5

THE HATCHET FALLS

Last-Ditch Efforts

Theodore Bell was fighting his own war within the state of California, where the legislature would consider the Eighteenth Amendment on January 13, 1919. He sued to get an injunction to freeze California's ratification of the amendment, in the desperate hope that other states would follow and the Wets could find some wiggle room. The suit failed. California's state legislature ratified the Eighteenth Amendment, the twenty-second state to do so. On January 16, 1919, Nebraska became the critical thirty-sixth state. With its acceptance of the amendment, three-fourths of the nation's states had passed it, and over the next few weeks, ten more would vote in its favor. New Jersey was the last to ratify in favor of Prohibition, accepting the amendment on March 9, 1922. Only Connecticut and Rhode Island rejected it. It would go into effect a year and a day after Nebraska's ratification: January 17, 1920. The Eighteenth Amendment prohibited "the manufacture, sale, or transportation of intoxicating liquors within, the importation into, or the exportation thereof from the United States and all territory subject to the jurisdiction thereof for beverage purposes."

The amendment to outlaw alcohol was much more popular than its companion, the Nineteenth, which provided for women's suffrage. That landmark change began its way through the states in June 1919 and was

Eight local men expressed their desire to sweep away the hatchet (Prohibition) and ring the bell for Bell in this clever old snapshot. *Courtesy of Mark and Deborah Arrighi.*

finally completed on August 18, 1920. Some southern states didn't get around to accepting it until much later, including Florida (1969), Georgia (1970), Louisiana (1970), North Carolina (1971) South Carolina (1973) and Mississippi (1984).

Theodore Bell was the Napa Valley's version of Jude, the saint of desperate and lost causes. Despite Prohibition's overwhelming momentum, he persisted, or at least he was available to represent those who somehow believed there was a chance of stopping it. In August 1919, representing Calistoga vintner Ephraim Light, Bell argued to the California Supreme Court that wine should never have been included in Wilson's May 1917 war measures because grapes were not a commodity necessary to the war effort and did not need to be rationed. Wine should, therefore, be excluded from the language of the Eighteenth Amendment, and California should not have ratified it (nor should any of the states). He presented several experts who buttressed his argument that because no grains or sugar were involved in the vinification process, Wilson's inclusion of wine in war legislation made no sense. His argument did have merit; the ASL, therefore, sent some heavy hitters to argue against him, including an assistant U.S. attorney for the

Northern District of California, Annette Abbott Adams. Bell was unable to persuade the judiciary and lost yet again. Shortly thereafter, Adams became the first female assistant attorney general of the United States.

THE VOLSTEAD ACT

Accepting a new constitutional amendment was one thing; creating the means to enforce it was another. Since alcohol was necessary for some industrial purposes and for use in the liturgies of some religions, distinctions had to be drawn between recreational and non-recreational use of intoxicating beverages. An entirely new governmental agency needed to come together to give teeth and focus to Prohibition laws. In June 1919, chairman of the House Judiciary Committee Andrew Volstead, a Minnesota Progressive with a small face and a big mustache, presented the National Prohibition Act to Congress for its consideration and approval. Because Volstead introduced it, the proposed enabling legislation became known as the Volstead Act, but everyone knew it was the ASL's Wayne Wheeler who actually wrote it. Congress passed the Volstead Act on October 18, 1919.

Throughout his tumultuous second term, President Wilson had been preoccupied with concerns connected to the war in Europe, the creation of a League of Nations to prevent future wars and the fate of demobilized soldiers as they returned to the States, among other things. He himself suffered from the influenza virus at the start of 1919, and in September, he collapsed. A few weeks later, a stroke left him paralyzed on the right side and blind in one eye. When Congress passed the Volstead Act, he rose from his bed to veto it. He had never intended his emergency wartime measures to become permanent laws of the land, and he had been too distracted by the international crisis to identify the peril to democracy that had arisen at home during his watch. He vetoed the Volstead Act, but the next day, the House that the ASL had packed overrode his objection. He was too sick to fight back. He remained in office another two years, but his disability was profound, and he had no voice in the Prohibition empire that Wheeler and his cohorts were building behind his back.

Napa Valley growers and vintners pored over the language of the Volstead Act to find ways to keep their businesses alive. There were plenty of loopholes. Alcohol was still permissible in sacramental wines, some medicines and cider, as was denatured alcohol for industrial uses. Doctors could prescribe one pint of alcohol per patient per day for ten days. The most promising exception was that heads of households could make up to two hundred gallons of intoxicating beverage for their family's private use. The Internal Revenue Service was soon flooded with requests for permits from heads of families to produce wine. Permits were also available for transporting alcohol, and pharmacists filled out forms detailing their fulfillment of prescriptions for alcohol.

A number of wineries tried to get their wares certified as sacramental wines. The CWA plant at Greystone, for example, made up labels describing some of its products as altar wines, slapped them on bottles and shipped them. The law stipulated that special permits were necessary for wines to be considered sacramental or industrial, however, and only a few vintners received them. The CWA may have received one for religious use, but the market for altar wine was minuscule compared to the kind of volume the CWA was used to and depended on. The most important recipient of these rare licenses in the Napa Valley was Georges de Latour's Beaulieu in Rutherford. De Latour also procured a permit to manufacture, transport and sell wine as an additive in curing tobacco. Beringer Winery was another that received a license to sell sacramental wine, and to extend its options, it built fruit dehydrators to dry its grapes until it could find other uses for them. Nothing said it couldn't still grow grapes, although there were clauses in the fine print that warned against providing the means for others to make intoxicating substances.

The *Napa Daily Journal* reported in October 1919 that the Volstead Act would reduce the amount of alcohol permissible in beer to half of 1 percent— not enough to bother fermenting. Napa's *braumeister* George Blaufuss made preparations to brew cider. After his friend Joe Migliavacca bottled and kegged all the wine he could from his family's large Fifth Street winery, George bought the place from him. Napans in the alcohol business tended to be liberal in their support for one another, enduring a shared experience that helped them continue as a force in the small city's political life.

Wine lovers stocked up. Nathan Ghisolfo, proprietor of the Mount View Hotel in Calistoga, laid out his inventory on the barroom floor and sold every bottle at one dollar each, regardless of type. Flocks of buyers descended like starlings to snap up everything they could. St. Helena pioneer descendant Ina Hart told her biographer that her family bought as much as they could from their friends the Beringers and hid it in the back of their basement, walled in behind stacks of canned fruit, as if possessing wine were in itself a crime. The new law would not prohibit the possession of alcoholic products by private citizens for personal use, but given the anti-alcohol spirit of the

Venerable wineries like Castle Rock in the west Napa hills had to close because of Prohibition. *Courtesy of Yates Family Vineyard.*

times, the Harts might have feared criticism from teetotaling strangers who happened to pass through their basement.

The case was different for professional winemakers. All legal wineries were bonded and on record with the Treasury Department. To ensure that they did not continue their enterprises after January 17, the Treasury Department told each of them to inventory their unsold products. Most wineries aged their wine in huge fermentation tanks and sold it in puncheons (kegs containing 318.226432 liters) rather than bottles. Neither the puncheons nor the tanks were airtight, so the risk of spoiling was high if the product couldn't move in a timely fashion. Many found this to be a lot of work for much risk and little gain and simply destroyed everything they had on hand. D. Perry Doak, for example, poured rivers of Far Niente's red wine into the ground, although perhaps not all of his inventory, because he kept his winemaker Hans Hansen in his employ. Hans had learned winemaking from his father, Andrew, Benson's old superintendent, winemaker and Treasury Department proxy.

As the 1919 season matured, the grapes were looking especially good. Winemakers conceded that their skills were no longer needed, but growers found themselves in big demand. Caravans of trucks from the Bay Area bumped along the county road to fill up with ripe fruit, from which they hoped to make their own wine. Heads of household all over the country began ordering shipments of fresh grapes, but crates and railroad cars were in frustratingly short supply. Growers who could round up the means to transport their berries found themselves making better money than ever before. Grape prices rose to heights even greater than the CWA had paid in its best years.

FORNI'S CHICAGO CONNECTIONS

Charles Forni was about thirty when the Volstead Act passed and was bustling with energy. He had returned from Sink's vineyards to help with Lombarda Winery, which, despite all the labor and teamwork that had gone into its creation, was doing poorly because of management and quality problems, perhaps because winemaker and foreman Ted Arrighi had left to operate his own winery. Charles's uncle Antonio had died, and another relative was

Wines sold well in Chicago before Prohibition, and the area was a major market for fresh wine grapes after it began. *Courtesy Yates Family Vineyard.*

overseeing the winery operation. Charles did what he could to revive the place, but with the Volstead Act a given, Lombarda stopped making wine. Forni's relationship with Captain Gaetano Rossi bore fruit again. Rossi had relatives in Chicago who possessed a great love of wine. With Rossi's relatives as buyers, Charles Forni and a partner, Adam Bianchi, put together a shipment of thirty-two railroad cars full of fresh grapes. To ensure that the cargo arrived safely, Charles rode to Chicago along with the grapes. The adventure taught them that some grape varieties traveled better than others. Petite Sirah, for example, didn't hold up well, nor did Zinfandel, but Alicante Bouschet had thicker skin and was more resilient. They grafted and replanted, and others did the same. Alicante Bouschet became the dominant grape in the Napa Valley.

Ted Arrighi had purchased a defunct but spacious three-story stone facility called Alta Vista on the Ink Grade Road on the way to Pope Valley, far from the beaten path. The previous owner was an Englishman named Richards. Hillside vineyards came with the property, and Arrighi was producing significant amounts of bulk wine. Cars could barely navigate the road; teams of horses brought the wine to town in puncheons. Because his place was so far from the beaten path, Arrighi may have felt safe. He continued to make wine and sold it by the jug.

IT BEGINS

January 17, 1920, dawned cold and very, very dry, and with it came federal agents carrying chicken wire and padlocks for sequestering and impounding inventories of wine. They first visited large, well-known wineries like Inglenook, Larkmead and Ghisolfo. They measured the wine in the vats and kegs, counted whatever bottles remained and quarantined the product so that their owners were hard put to find ways to access their supply. (Most found ways to do so anyway.) They destroyed the distillery at Larkmead, even though the Salmina family had stopped producing alcohol several months earlier. Smaller, less obvious facilities like the Arrighis' and Nichelinis' escaped their notice, at least at first.

Debonair vintner Georges de Latour prepared himself for the invasion of Prohibition by working with the enemy. His friend Archbishop Riordan had passed away, and he grew close to the succeeding archbishop, Edward Joseph Hanna. With Hanna's endorsement, the Prohibition Department granted de

Latour a permit to make, sell and transport altar wine. With a marketing office already established in New York City, Beaulieu wines showed up in churches everywhere, and the winery made money hand over fist. The demand outpaced his supply of grapes. He bought or leased Wente Brothers winery, which did not have a license to produce altar wine; this relationship allowed that Livermore winery to survive Prohibition, although technically it did not operate during the 1920s. De Latour extended Catholic clergymen everywhere an open invitation to visit his winery and built a guest cottage in the middle of a vineyard with an altar where they could conduct private Masses. The cottage was near his chateau-like home and fitted with amenities that may have matched his guests' secret longings for the trappings of aristocratic Europe. There he and his staff could close deals for sacramental wine by the carload.

German-speaking, Kaiser-toasting Theodore Gier took the opposite approach. He wanted nothing to do with Prohibition and may have believed himself to be above the law. He continued to make, sell and transport wine after the Eighteenth Amendment became law. He was arrested in February 1920, just weeks after Prohibition officially began. Thirty witnesses testified that he had moved more than two hundred barrels of wine and fifty gallons of sherry to his Oakland warehouse for consolidation and sale. His lawyers managed to delay the procedures as well as the final ruling, but when the skein of his arguments ran out, he was fined $1,500, stripped of his license to make any kind of wine at all and sentenced to three months in the Alameda County jail. It was actually a light sentence, but he complained about the amenities in his cell. The warden allowed his wife to bring extra pillows and blankets, but he had to do his time just like the other prisoners.

To the Drys Gier was a perfect scapegoat: unflinchingly German, rich and a brewer of hard liquor as well as wine. A reporter went to interview him at the jail during a lunch break, when the guards were handing him a plate of stew and a piece of bread—hardly the kind of fare he was used to. "I did not anticipate any such fate as this," Gier told the reporter, "but I'm going to play the game like a sport." And he may indeed have thought the whole thing was some kind of game. When he was released, he immediately went back into the wine business—accidentally, or so he claimed. He crushed 100,000 gallons of fresh grapes during the next harvest and included, he said, an additive that would keep it from fermenting. The juice somehow fermented anyway, and the feds discovered it right away. They confiscated the wine and fined him sixteen cents a gallon. To pay his fines and make ends meet, he had to sell almost all of his assets, but he managed to retain Sequoia in the West Napa hills for the rest of the decade.

#21   #57

Monticello

Monticello, Cal,
May 10 1920

Mr. Joseph Harris
Sheriff Napa Cal.

Friend Joe. — Virgil Anderson has rented the Hotel here, and it is reported that several good times, drinking wine, have gone on about the place. I am told that a jug of wine is placed or hidden, and the fellows put wise as to where it is, so they just help themselves. Whether Anderson buys the wine, and sells it I do not know. It is possible someone donates the wine and uses the Hotel for a meeting place to drink and have a good time.

There is no question, but what the wine comes from Niolinus. If the revenue men would get busy, and put the lid on him, I am satisfied drinking would end here.

Yours Respectfully
Clifford Clark

Clifford Clark snitched on patrons of a Monticello hotel in 1920. *Courtesy of the Napa County Historical Society.*

Gier's prosecution seemed to satisfy the Treasury Department for a while. They turned their energies elsewhere and left Volstead enforcement to the local sheriff and police departments. No one seemed to have much enthusiasm for arresting violators in the Napa Valley. The papers occasionally reported arrests in nearby Sonoma County, but throughout the rest of 1920 and nearly all of 1921 a curtain seemed to drop over the wine country. The *Napa Daily Journal* sometimes printed news of potential interest to its Wet readers, like the July 29, 1922 item that happened to mention that "Deputy IRS Collector Edward M. Kelly and his wife and her mother" were here "checking Napa County wineries." Other checkers were also here, the paper blandly commented. In order to enter places where they suspected intoxicating beverages might be made, agents had to obtain warrants. County staff telephoned the intended targets. With warnings like this, bootleggers knew to hide their operations when the law was around.

Wine was still available, of course, and the Drys in the county's various communities weren't happy about it. Clifford Clark, a resident of Monticello (now under Lake Berryessa), was miffed that men gathering at the town's hotel took breaks from their meeting to quaff from a bottle labeled "Nichelini." He complained in a letter to Sheriff Harris, "If the revenue men would get busy, and put the lid on him, I am satisfied that drinking would end here."

THE MEDICAL EXCEPTION

A tweak in the Prohibition law occurred in the beginning of 1921: physicians were no longer limited to prescribing intoxicating beverages in pints. Ailing patients could now consume as much as the doctor felt was necessary. Remedies "for medicinal purposes only" could be picked up at drugstores. Doctors would get $3 for each prescription they wrote for alcohol, of which they were allowed four hundred a year. Given that the average doctor only made about $1,200 a year, writing prescriptions would almost double their income. Wine was not included. Inspired nevertheless, Theodore Bell hosted a big social event at his home right after the news broke. The *St. Helena Star* published the names of some of the guests. Among others, they included two local medical doctors, a local dentist, a local pharmacist and the town postmaster, who also ran a general store. Also invited were the president of Portland Cement (whose Napa Junction plant was still in business), the San Francisco fire commissioner and the San Francisco district attorney, two

The medical exception may have prompted some of Napa's leading citizens to conspire. A gentlemen's outing at Dr. Hennesey's ranch included (top row, left to right) City Attorney John York, Justice of the Peace George Johnson, unknown, Dave Wilson, unknown, unknown, Charles Cather, Dr. Leslie Stern, Julius Goodman, Joe "Pills" Levinson; (middle row, left to right) unknown, Theodore Gier (?), Dr. Charles Hackett, Dr. E.Z. Hennesey, Billby Wilson, Frank Mackinder, Dave Cavagnaro; (on ground) Abe Strauss, Charles Levinson. *Courtesy of John York.*

officials from an import/export company, a wealthy stockbroker, a famous chef who was also an expert on wine and Bismarck Bruck, the district's state assemblyman. Bell's brother Ed, defender of justice for those accused of alcohol-related crimes and by now an attorney in Oakland, was probably there too. Speculation ensued that these gentlemen actually gathered to discuss the legal and extralegal ramifications of the new medical exception and how it might benefit them. Why not? Perhaps this loophole could work to everyone's advantage, especially if trains and ships were somehow involved and officials could be paid to look the other way. With five Catholics for every one Protestant and therefore overwhelmingly Wet, San Francisco politicians could hardly be expected to toe the line.

In the cat-and-mouse game that was to ensue, there were far more mice than cats in Northern California. The Treasury Department had fewer than 3,500 agents patrolling the entire nation, and they had plenty of work to do in eastern cities, where a new criminal element was starting to create mayhem. Most of these lawbreakers were members of the immigrant groups the Protestant majority had rejected.

A few "T-men" were available for duty in the Napa Valley. They may not have been deployed wisely, at least at first. The Ghisolfos' experience was a case in point. Despite the fact that the Ghisolfos had practically given away their inventory at the Mount View Hotel, the Treasury Department was convinced that they were bootleggers. Patriarch Nathan Ghisolfo did have a fairly large winery, and there was still wine there in vats and barrels. The feds measured their wine and found a discrepancy between the amount they said they had on hand at the start of Prohibition and the amount that was there a short time later. The Ghisolfos claimed that some of the wine had evaporated, but the U.S. marshal was sure there was evil afoot. He placed two agents at the Ghisolfos' residence, where they moved in and made themselves at home. As the months rolled by and nothing much had changed, the Ghisolfo family petitioned to have the agents removed. The marshal refused and ordered that their wine be destroyed. There was no law against having large amounts of wine on hand if it had been created before Prohibition officially began; it was just illegal to make more than two hundred gallons of it, sell it or transport it anywhere. Tired of being bullied, Nathan sought and received a court order to delay and hopefully stop the destruction of his wine. It would be a long time before he got an answer. In the meantime, his wine stayed.

BEER IN NAPA

After a year of denying themselves the beverages they had always consumed with their meals and at parties, many Napans grew weary of Prohibition very quickly. Dave Cavagnaro, the popular proprietor of a bar in East Napa called the Brooklyn Hotel, met with his friend and former *braumeister* George Blaufuss and told George, "This county's drying up. Why don't you brew some beer? We could all use some good medicine."

"But what about the police?" asked George.

"We are the police," said Dave. "We'll fix everything. How much will it cost to start up?"

George thought for a moment. "I'll need hops, malt, bottles, labels…"

"No labels!" said Dave.

Dave's brother Henry, aka "Punch," was a Napa policeman. Between the newspaper, the telephone, friendly police like Punch and word of mouth, it might be safe to go back into the beer business if it could be done discreetly, especially since the Wet Percy King had replaced Henry Gesford as the lead judge of the Napa Superior Court. The Prohibition commissioner, pioneer descendant James M. Palmer, was a Napa attorney with many friends in town. He had been a member of the state assembly from 1912 to 1914. His sister was married to a Migliavacca, and he had once worked for John E. Walden, editor of the Wet-friendly *Napa Journal*. As a general agent for the Bureau of Internal Revenue, he could issue and sign permits for medicinal alcohol, hear cases and order fines or refer them to a higher court. Even if King or Palmer knew about an illicit operation like the Blaufuss Brewery— and it is fairly clear they did know, because the air in town was pungent with the smell of brewing beer—they didn't need to do anything about it unless an arrest was actually involved.

The golden river was soon flowing at Cavagnaro's Brooklyn Hotel. Public officials and regular citizens showed up there once again with their empty kegs and pitchers, and the aroma of fermentation flowered the air. There were still plenty of Drys in Napa, and the activity at the brewery did not go unnoticed. The feds leveled their sights on George Blaufuss. When Punch Cavagnaro learned there would be a raid at the brewery, he told Dave, and Dave told George. The Blaufusses were terrified and sought help from city attorney Wally Rutherford, one of his regular customers. "Don't worry," Rutherford told them. "We'll fix everything."

The Blaufusses and their friends spent the night trying to bottle as much beer as they could. They hid it in caches all over Napa (including a water tank behind Dave's bar and a barn at the state hospital), but the brew that was still fermenting couldn't be concealed and was too unstable to bottle. Treasury agents collared George the next afternoon and charged him with "having in possession and unlawfully manufacturing liquor more commonly known as beer, and containing more than one half of one percent of alcohol by volume." The penalty for this could be up to $10,000 and five years in jail. Lacking the resources of the affluent Theodore Gier, Blaufuss feared the worst. Two of his friends posted his $1,000 bail, and he went home to worry.

Commissioner Palmer would hear the case the next day. It was clear Blaufuss was guilty. Palmer would have to send him to Sacramento for sentencing, and the penalty could be as steep as the one given to Gier, something the middle-class Blaufuss family could ill afford. Judge Percy King quickly interceded. He heard the case, found against the defendant, charged him $200 and ordered him to dispose of the remaining beer by pouring it into the Napa River. King also told him to make restitution by donating two hundred cases of bottled beer to the Veterans Home at the Presidio in San Francisco and the Veterans Hospital in Palo Alto—to be used for medicinal purposes, of course.

STILLS

The closure of the resurrected Blaufuss brewery was as disappointing to the city's drinkers as it was to the Blaufusses themselves and drove quite a few to take matters into their own hands. Beer wasn't hard to make, but acquiring the proper ingredients for a good brew was difficult, since hops and barley farmers were now rare. Making hard liquor was a lot easier. All that was needed was a still and some jugs. As Mary and Antone Ghirardi had discovered in Yountville, a still required a source of cool water, a source of intense heat, two metal vessels (copper or tin) and some coiled metal pipes.

The prospective distiller poured the substance to be distilled into the first vessel. Distilled wine would become brandy, but water and mashes of sugar, rotting corn, wheat or even potatoes would also work. The first vessel was placed over a hot fire and allowed to come to a steaming boil. The distiller placed a metal bulb over the first vessel, and if it wasn't threaded to screw onto the pot below, the distiller could seal the two together with strips of cloth dipped in a simple paste of flour and water. (The bulb was helpful because the heated mash foamed, and extra space was necessary to keep it from boiling over onto the fire.) A narrow tube connected to the top of the bulb caught the steam from the boiling brew and conveyed it into a second vessel a foot or two away. To increase the length of the tube, it was coiled at the end. Cold water in the second vessel cooled the evaporated material in the tubing and returned it to a clear liquid. The far end of the tubing met a spigot that would allow the distillation in the tubing to exit the second vessel. The first ounce or two of the liquid, called the "heads," was considered too crude to drink, and it was discarded. A highly alcoholic substance then followed, and as the mash in the first vessel boiled down, liquid with ever-decreasing amounts of alcohol followed. The distiller collected everything but the heads, cleaned out the apparatus and ran the alcohol through the still again to homogenize it. Some distillers aged their product in barrels charred to impart added flavor, but most home distillers were more than ready to use or sell what the process had created as soon as they could.

Before it was destroyed by federal agents, this still set-up could brew whiskey. The can on the left had a sealed top with a pipe extending from it to the other can. The coil added length to the pipe between the hot chamber and the cool one.

Lots could go wrong. Foam containing particulates of the matter being distilled could collect in the tubing and block the flow of the steam, which could back up and cause the bulb to explode off the vessel beneath it. So much high-test alcohol so close to such intense heat was inflammable. Exploding stills became commonplace, especially in East Napa, where the population of Italians was especially dense. When the volunteer fire department blew its whistle, it used a code to describe where in town a fire was. When the East Napa code went off—which it often did—citizens would say, "There goes another still."

Chapter 6

CHAOS

DEATH ON THE ROAD

It was no secret that intoxicating beverages could be found in the Napa Valley during Prohibition. They were available by the glass, the bottle or the jug. The *Star* described the "droves and swarms" of autos rumbling up the unpaved highway to St. Helena—so many that Highway 29 gained a reputation as the second-most traveled road in California. Accidents, often fatal ones, became commonplace, especially after dark, when drivers had drunk their fill. Many cars lacked adequate headlights, so to reduce the carnage, laws were written requiring adequate equipment for night driving. Laws regarding drunk driving weren't considered. Technically, there was no such thing anymore.

The City of St. Helena bought acreage west of the county road and south of the town to serve as a campground and resting place for those too intoxicated to navigate their vehicles. (It also became a place where they could purchase more liquor.) Part of it became known as Crane Park, for the pioneer physician/winemaker George Crane, who once owned the land. There was a similar park in Napa as well. South of Napa, on Highway 121 heading toward Sonoma County, there was a treacherous S-shaped stretch that saw so many accidents it became known as "Death Curve."

It was a nighttime traffic accident—or the appearance of one—that took the life of the Napa Valley's favorite son in September 1922. According to

Above: Tourists (and locals) risked flat tires on Napa County's unpaved roads. Tourists seeking alcohol swarmed the area in the early and mid-1920s. *Courtesy of Sandra Learned Perry.*

Left: Theodore Bell dedicated himself to stopping and then circumventing Prohibition. He died under suspicious circumstances.

the *Star*, Theodore Bell had gone to celebrate Labor Day at the Lagunitas Rod and Gun Club, a woodsy resort in the unincorporated wilds of western Marin County, not far from the coast. The area had a romantic past, replete with tales of highwaymen and stagecoach robbers. Its upscale members had gone there for many years to hunt, fish and partake of the outdoors, but in 1917, the clubhouse was flooded, and much of that ceased; thus, Bell's weekend there was hard to explain. The roads in the area were especially dangerous—unlit, not well maintained, hilly and winding.

Bell's chauffeur said he was driving Bell back to his home in San Francisco. According to his testimony, he was trying to pass a car on the Bolinas Grade, two miles from Fairfax, when another car suddenly appeared coming from the other direction. The chauffeur swerved to avoid it, and Bell's car plunged off a forty-foot embankment. Bell died instantly. The other car sped away. Many things in the chauffeur's story seemed suspicious, including the fact that he himself was only slightly injured. As after the big party earlier in the year, rumors regarding the true cause of the accident were rampant. The place where the accident occurred was convenient to whiskey smugglers coming in from the coast. Had Bell been complicit in establishing a bootlegging ring? Had competing criminals snuffed him out? Were Treasury agents in the other car? Or was it a super-patriot, still angry about Bell's ties to the Church of the Living God? Or a dedicated Dry who believed Bell was in league with the devil? The questions were never answered. If there really was a car coming in the other direction, the driver may have gotten away with murder.

CITIZENS ARRESTED

In October 1922, not long after Bell's funeral, the Treasury Department returned to the Napa Valley and conducted a sting. They lured a former Oakville vintner named Arnold Regnier and his wife into selling them five gallons of wine for ten dollars. The defendants claimed that they thought the money was for the good time these "guests" had at their home and former winery. Judge Palmer thought otherwise. He forgave the wife but sent the husband to Sacramento for sentencing.

In November 1922, the California legislature passed the Wright Act, the state's version of the Volstead Act. It mandated law enforcement officials to carry out the terms of the national law. There would be no more looking the other way. Law enforcement personnel failing to carry out the terms of the Volstead Act would be prosecuted. Unwilling to arrest his friends and neighbors, the Napa police chief, Charles Otterson, quit. Sheriff Joe Harris stayed on and in 1923 arrested another Oakville man, Andy Bartolucci, who allegedly sold wine and brandy to the patrons of his small restaurant (a former winery). Alcohol was found and confiscated, but the family was able to get the charges dismissed. The Bartoluccis were fairly well known. Andy (short for Andrea) immigrated to America from Italy in 1913 and went to work in a quicksilver mine in Pope Valley. He sent for his wife, Guglielma, and son Louis in 1919. By 1920, he and the family were living in St. Helena, and in 1923, he was somehow able to purchase the Oakville home and defunct winery of August Jeanmonod at a public auction for $14,250. A service station was also on the property. How he was able to acquire so much money so quickly is unknown, and how he managed to get the charges dropped is also unknown, but it may have been a good sign for others. The following year, the house and winery burned down, taking the service station with it as well as the family's almost new Dodge touring car. Seeming to take this disaster in stride, they moved into the larger home of deceased vintner Adolph Brun, co-owner of the former Nouveau Medoc winery.

Sheriff Harris turned his sights on St. Helena. Just after Christmas, he caught Maurizio Mori at the Depot Saloon selling alcohol; he also nabbed the proprietor of the Hotel St. Helena, who resisted arrest at first. He then arrested Silvio Pastorino, an employee at the William Tell Hotel, for the same thing. Pastorino sprinted out the back door, but Harris chased him down. Pastorino had to pay $450. None of the St. Helena men got off the hook or received the leniency Percy King had given George Blaufuss. A pattern was beginning to emerge: unless the violations were especially egregious, it seemed like well-known citizens or those in good standing with officials in the county seat got better deals than others did.

Tourists came in dilapidated flivvers or in nice touring cars up the unpaved road to St. Helena. They arrived with empty jugs and left with full ones. Their complaints about the poor condition of Highway 29 resulted in it getting paved for the first time, around 1923. They bought wine, but most of the illicit sales that took place were of moonshine, the product of stills hidden away in the rugged hills that straddled both sides of the valley. Alcohol was so plentiful that outsiders began to assume that everyone in Napa County kept cases of hooch in their garages. There was a rash of break-ins, and the newspaper warned residents to lock their garages. Attempted thefts, some of them at gunpoint, continued throughout the 1920s. Knowing that

Beaulieu was still in the wine business, five "tourists" drove up to the winery one evening, accosted a worker and demanded that he turn over some wine to them. The worker hailed the night watchman, who grabbed a shotgun and fired at them. They fled. A few days later, de Latour reported that eight barrels of wine were missing from the inventory. Although the local police found and arrested the thwarted thieves, the barrels never showed up. Had the wily French vintner seized yet another good business opportunity? The practice of reporting bogus burglaries became somewhat common among vintners wishing to conceal the depletion of their inventory. In fact, wine theft was something of a blessing for de Latour, and it occurred rather often, a function of how widely distributed his products were. The net result was that the rectory/church/diocese whose supply had been pilfered merely ordered some more.

Dishonest tourists were a problem for small bootleggers as well. Steven Jackse had a winery at the site of today's Napa Valley Vintners Association building. After filling a customer's trunk with wine jugs, the customer drove off without paying. Jackse complained to his friends, but he could hardly complain to the police.

Sheriff Harris had plenty of work to do throughout 1923 and '24 without needing to sift through fake police reports, let alone thefts of bootleg. He found a treasure-trove of fine wines and whiskeys in Calistoga in the summer of 1923 and hauled it down to the courthouse in Napa, where he displayed it on the lawn. Nine barrels of wine, several dozen bottles of liquor and a case of "real Scotch whiskey" reminded passersby of what they'd been missing lately. The suspected accomplices in this bootlegging plot were found guilty and were fined a total of $6,600. Among them were a young Calistogan, Joe Nolasco, as well as Joe Baldocchi, A. Negri and Maurizio Mori, the latter having already met Harris's handcuffs once before. Negri may well have been Anecito Negri, who was brazen enough to list his occupation as a saloonkeeper in Napa Junction on the 1920 census, after Prohibition had already begun.

Also arrested in this ring was the Italian Swiss vintner Anton Nichelini. The Nichelinis were still very much in the business of making, transporting and selling wine. Their remote eastern hills location was so far off the beaten path that they had no telephone (no electricity either), so they lacked the advantage of the warning call from Punch Cavagnaro or others who knew about busts in advance. To conceal their illicit product from the law's prying eyes, Anton had taken to crushing grapes at the old wooden winery up the hill, fermenting and storing the juice there and conveying it,

Above: Bill and Anton Nichelini turned to bootlegging to survive Prohibition. *Courtesy of Doug Patterson.*

Opposite, top: The Pocai Winery in Calistoga was one of the few to remain in production, if clandestine, throughout much of Prohibition. *Courtesy of the Napa Valley Wine Library Association.*

Opposite, bottom: Anton and Caterina Nichelini posed for this picture in July 1920 with their eight children, two daughters-in-law and two granddaughters. Anton had no intention of quitting the wine industry. *Courtesy of Doug Patterson.*

in limited quantities, down to the larger stone building below, using pipes in the ground. A water pipe ran in conjunction with the wine pipe, and if a Volstead emergency arose, he could turn a valve so that water ran from the pipe and not wine.

Harris was certain that the 1923 arrest had failed to dissuade Anton and his Italian and Italian Swiss friends from their lives of crime, and he was right. Rumors were circulating that Anton's son Bill was serving as personal bootlegger to San Francisco's booze-swigging mayor, "Sunny Jim" Rolph. (Napa's Dave Cavagnaro was also close to Sunny Jim, and it's probable that the mayor and eventual California governor had several reliable sources for alcohol products.) After repeal, Rolph's limousine found its way to the Nichelini winery. The wooden floorboards were removable, providing plenty of space for the temporary storage of contraband between Chiles Valley and San Francisco.

Calistoga proved to be ripe for the plucking in 1923. Harris hauled in several restaurant owners and waiters. Giuseppe Musante, owner of a former bar near the train station, advertised "soft drinks" in the city directory but also had the other kind. Pete Pizzuti sold the other kind at his Fior D'Italia Hotel at 302 Lincoln, as did A. Brenta at his Swiss Chalet on Highway 29. They were all caught and fined. Peter Molo's Monte Carlo "resort" on Diamond Mountain Road apparently offered illicit entertainment along with the illegal refreshments. Molo was closed down, but he resurfaced several times and became a repeat offender without an influential sponsor to keep his name out of the newspapers.

Rose Nichelini hunted rabbits to help keep food on the table. *Courtesy of Doug Patterson.*

As in Napa, stills abounded in out-of-the-way places up valley. In August 1923, Sheriff Harris found a "Mrs. M.H. Evits" operating two modest stills off the Oat Hill Mine Road in a remote section of Calistoga, one with a five-gallon capacity and the other a ten-gallon. (There was a Mary Evetts living near Soda Springs in Napa at the time, but no M.H. Evits is listed in the Census.)

Sheriff Harris and his federal counterparts continued to keep an eye on Anton Nichelini for the next several months. A federal agent's notes reveal

Report of Operator J. W. Payne,

A. Nichelini

Jan, 8th, 1924 at 1.25 o'clock P.M.

On the above mentioned date Payne visited the place of Nichelini in ~~Chiles~~ Sage Canyon, and purchased from Mrs Nichelini, (old lady) two gallons of red wine paying therefore the sum of $3.00. A party known as "Dutch" accompanyed Payne on this trip and was a witness to the buy and the paying for same by Payne.

Feb, 15th, 1924, at 2.20 o'clock P.M.

On this date Payne visited the Nichelini place again, in company with Mr Price, and purchased one gallon of red wine, paying therefore $1.50

Price witnessed the buy and the paying for the wine by Payne. This buy was made from Mrs Nichelini.

Feby, 19th, 1924 at 4.40 0'clock P.M.

On this date Payne visited the Nichelini place again in company with ~~J.W.Scallen~~ and purchased from from Mr Nichelini one gallon of red wine paying there fore the sum of $1.50, She was always in the habit of selling this wine for $100 per gallon and charging $.50 for the jug, making the buy $1.50 for all.

Federal agent J.W. Payne kept notes on his arrest of Anton Nichelini. *Courtesy of Napa County Historical Society.*

that Operator J.W. Payne had come by at 1:25 p.m. on January 8, 1924, with a "friend" (another agent) and purchased some wine from Caterina Nichelini. He came again at 2:20 p.m. a few weeks later with a different friend and bought again from Caterina. He visited at 4:40 p.m. with a third friend a few days later and bought again from her. He showed up again at 6:00 that evening, and this time Anton was home and sold him some wine. The agents may have been milking Caterina for information; their real target, however, was Anton. They arrested him and took him to the St. Helena jail, located on the site of today's St. Helena Parochial School.

The 1924 arrest of Anton Nichelini was part of a major bust that netted twenty-two people in all, some of them very well-known names. Included was the discovery of a huge distillery off Ink Grade Road in Angwin with six large stills and equipment and inventory worth many thousands of dollars. The facility was built next to a cold stream, which not only provided a steady source of water for cooling but also served as a trail the bootleggers could use to conceal their comings and goings. Darrell Samuels, whose wife was an Arrighi, and Harold Stevens, a Vallejo taxi driver, were caught red-handed on the premises. Pioneer descendant Charles Tucker and grape growers Joe Bianchi and Joe Yudnich were also among them.

The feds also arrested Ted Arrighi. The Arrighis' winery was close by, and it would have been convenient for Ted to dispose of some of his unsold wine inventory by getting it converted to brandy. In a 1979 interview, Arrighi's youngest daughter, Inez McManus, told the historian William Heintz that she remembered her father having some 30,000 gallons of wine to sell during Prohibition. She said he was waiting for someone to take it for $1.10 a gallon, but the man never came, and he finally got rid of the wine "because it soured." Conversion into brandy was an ideal way for getting rid of over-the-hill wine. The Arrighis' winery was estimated to have a capacity of 100,000 gallons, and Inez believed that he sold all the wine he made during Prohibition. People bought it by the gallon—without labels, of course.

A branch of the Arrighi family that spelled their name with one "r"—Arighi—lived in St. Helena on Tainter Street. Bill Arighi and his brother Amile both ran drugstores, Bill at 1302 Main in St. Helena and Amile at 949 Brown in Napa. A relative named Ernest Ballarini helped finance them. The brothers entered the pharmacy business sometime around 1915, well before Prohibition, and there is no evidence that they engaged in any illegal activities. It would have been tempting, however, for the Arighi brothers to consider the benefits of a clandestine partnership with their cousins, since beside churches, drugstores were the only places where alcohol could be acquired more or less legally. Young Mario Vasconi went to work for Bill in the St. Helena store and eventually became a licensed pharmacist as well (and, later, owner of the store).

Similarly, a member of the pioneering Levinson family in Napa had also established a drugstore. Joe Levinson—whom many affectionately called "Pills"—was a close, lifelong friend of a popular Napa doctor, E.Z. Hennessey, MD. Hennessey lived large, as did the Levinsons. There is no reason to believe that Hennessey would have tolerated abstinence from alcohol and good reason to suspect that he was more than liberal in writing prescriptions for thirsty Napans. Again, there is no known evidence of wrongdoing on the part of Levinson or Hennessey; if any of these important Napans were arrested, the newspapers made no mention of it.

Some familiar people did make the Napa papers in the summer of 1924, thanks to Sheriff Harris. Scandal-ridden industrialist D. Perry Doak had died in 1921, and his new wife, Frieda, stayed on at the old Far Niente estate with her daughter Elizabeth. Bad press involving the Doaks continued even after D. Perry's death. His mother, Sarah, tried to get the court to nullify his will and have the estate willed to herself instead of to Frieda, on the grounds that Frieda had unduly influenced him during his fatal illness. The judge ruled for Frieda, which enraged Sarah. Winemaker Hans Hansen continued to work at Far Niente, a position he had held since 1917. Harris discovered that Hansen was operating a still on an undeveloped parcel of land he owned off Soscol Avenue. Eleven people were implicated in the operation. Hansen was fined and ordered to spend five months in jail. Did a vengeful Sarah Doak rat on him? If Hansen used the still to satisfy his employer's needs, it would make sense that Frieda would have bailed him out.

Frieda was not one to let the grass grow under her feet. She entered into a romantic liaison with a retired (and married) marine colonel, John F. McGill, who shed his wife, Grace, and made it official with Frieda. McGill was the commander in charge of marines recruitment for the western states—a powerful man with far-reaching influence. Not long after their marriage, he and Frieda invited the new president of the United States, Calvin Coolidge, to visit their magnificent home in the former wine country. Coolidge declined. McGill and Frieda were both heavy drinkers, and their invitation to Coolidge somehow made it into the papers. It may have been a public relations ploy. With such apparently irreproachable connections, no one seemed to bother them much when they installed a private airstrip on their Oakville property. Every year from 1925 to 1929, another strip was added, each heading in a different direction. The Associated Oil Company erected a hangar there, painted in its company colors (red, green and cream) with "Oakville" written on the maroon roof. The airport was very busy throughout Prohibition.

One of Sheriff Harris's most lucrative Calistoga hauls occurred just before Thanksgiving 1924, when he raided the Hotel Calistoga, which also served as the town's post office. They arrested the manager, Bernard F. Hughes, who was also the assistant postmaster. The postmaster and owner of the hotel, Owen Kenny, happened to be in San Francisco for the evening. He received a phone call ordering him to report to Napa to be arraigned. Harris's men inventoried one thousand bottles of wine, two barrels of vermouth, two barrels of crème de menthe, eight hundred bottles of chianti and champagne and seven hundred barrels of red and white table wine, most of which they took to Switzer's warehouse on Laurel Street in Napa. They opened the bottles, cracked the barrels and poured almost everything on the ground behind Switzer's. (Not all of it made it to Switzer's—some pilfering occurred along the way.) The Hotel Calistoga was ordered to shut down. Kenny lost his job as postmaster, and he was probably hauled off to jail. Calistogans were overwhelmingly supportive of the Kennys and their plight. The hotel was still operating four months later when the Rotarians and their wives, the Ropals, held a special dinner there to which outsiders were not invited. Editor Charles Carroll of the *Weekly Calistogian* wrote that "Mrs. Kenny went on with the preparations, notwithstanding her recent bereavement…Much heartfelt sympathy was felt for her, together with a feeling of admiration for her grit to go through with it."

DAGO MARY'S

The biggest raid of Joe Harris's career took place in 1925 in Napa Junction, the rowdy little train stop just five miles north of Mare Island. It was there that the Negri family and "Dago Mary" had a very popular speakeasy. With the help of an informant (Emil Pedrini, who was in jail for bootlegging), Harris and two special agents, the Mastalatto brothers, choreographed a nighttime bust. A squad of sheriff cars crept up to the place with their lights off, and the cops broke into two groups. One crashed through the front door and confronted a room full of cigarette smoke and men enjoying various states of intoxication. A few of them jumped out the window and got away, but the rest—among them some of Napa's leading citizens—got nabbed.

The other team burst in through the back door and found Mary herself preparing food in the kitchen. She threw everything she could get her hands on at the sheriff's men, including knives, forks, pots and pans, glassware, crockery and small appliances, before they were able to subdue her and pack her into the paddy wagon with her many guests. The bust brought in thirty-five people, three of them women.

One of the arrested was Dave Cavagnaro, owner of the popular Brooklyn Hotel in East Napa and regarded by many as Italian Town's unofficial mayor. He paid his own fine of $900 and the fines of many who couldn't as well. Warrants were issued for the arrest of the few who got away—Fortunato Martini (owner of the Union Hotel), his brother-in-law Joe Tamburelli (owner of the Depot Restaurant), Eugene Venturino (Roma Hotel) and Leslie Brisbin. They were eventually rounded up too, and the financial burden of their stiff fines was difficult for them.

In February 1926, someone telephoned Venturino and Tamburelli to warn them that the Mastalatto brothers were coming to pay them an unwelcome visit. Tamburelli was able to hide the bootleg and avoided further trouble, but Venturino chose to defend his castle, the Roma Hotel. A fight broke out in the kitchen, during which one of the Mastalattos dropped a gun on the floor. All they netted was a single pint of liquor, for which Venturino was arrested—wrongly— and immediately released. The situation could easily have turned deadly.

It was no fun getting arrested. Owen Kenny and his wife, for example, were trembling with fear at the prospect of big fines and time in jail. Good citizens like Gier, Kenny, Arrighi, Nichelini and Hansen were often thrown into the same mix with questionable ones like Molo and repeat offender Andy Zadrow and in some cases stripped of their livelihood. A lien was placed on Joe Tamburelli's Depot Restaurant, and he was unable to borrow money when he needed it two years after the bust. Emma Fetters of Fetters Hot Springs in Sonoma was so upset by her experience getting busted at a speakeasy on Fourth Street that she died two weeks later.

There was another death in 1926 that dismayed many in the Napa Valley: Bismarck Bruck passed away of heart failure. The funeral was possibly the largest the city of St. Helena had ever experienced. Bruck had served three terms in the state assembly, was president of the board of supervisors, grand president of the Native Sons and president of Charles Krug Winery and the Bruck Juice Company. Frank Coombs, who had reentered politics after Bell's death, authored a resolution for the state assembly honoring Bruck's life and work. Activity ceased at the old Krug facility.

THE KKK

While some of the otherwise good citizens of the Napa Valley were sampling life on the wrong side of the law, another segment of the population was involved in an activity that was perfectly legal at the time: the Ku Klux Klan. Klansmen enjoyed dramatic displays of fire in the dark and scary rituals with horsemen and crosses. They also loved giving speeches and did so with vigor against the usual mainline targets—Catholics and Jews—as well as African Americans and people who drank alcohol, all of whom they characterized as amoral lawbreakers. In 1923, some two thousand people gathered under the moonlight in a field near Napa State Hospital to watch one hundred men in hoods and robes be initiated into the group. Many of the newly minted Klansmen were sailors from Mare Island. The KKK identified the Napa Valley as an untapped reservoir for new initiates. While their neighbors were getting arrested for Volstead offenses, those who agreed with the Drys (as well as those who believed in obeying unpopular laws) felt increasingly uncomfortable about the way the world seemed to be deteriorating before their very eyes. The fact that so many of the men and women caught in Joe Harris's net were Italian and Irish seemed to confirm the faith- and ethnicity-based prejudices that had long flecked the character of nativists throughout the country.

The Klan wooed this new resource with a fire-and-night extravaganza held in a field south of St. Helena in August 1924. They chartered a special train on the electric line that ran parallel to Highway 29 and provided parking for more than two thousand cars packed with the curious as well as the convinced. Only sixty new members were embraced into the white-sheeted bosom of the brotherhood, but between eight and ten thousand watched the ceremony, which ended with words of warning from a leading Klansman. If there were any bootleggers in the audience, the hooded knight promised, "The Klan will get you!" A few months later, the Klan held a similar rally in Calistoga, but only eleven people showed up. The Klan blamed it on the weather. They presented the public library with a Bible and went on their way.

One Klansman, a Napan named Charles Brisbin who lived on Eggleston Street (no known relation to Leslie Brisbin, one of Dago Mary's patrons), ran for city council in 1926. He garnered a lot of votes early in the election (the results apparently being public knowledge during the election process), which some attributed to the KKK. He told a reporter from the *Napa Journal* that it was his good friends in the neighborhood (many of them Italian) who caused the surge. "Well, why shouldn't I have friends?" he asked the reporter. "I ain't never done nothing to have enemies." He lost. The Klan maintained a small but occasionally menacing membership in the Napa Valley that endured long after Prohibition was over.

Meanwhile, some at the opposite end of the social and intellectual spectrum looked with dismay not only at the numerous arrests of ordinary American citizens but also at the wave of truly violent crime that was washing across the country, especially in New York and Chicago. While many in the upper echelons of American society supported Prohibition at first, they also liked their liquor as well as their wine and champagne. Alcoholism was rampant among the wealthy, but as exemplified by the Rosenbaums' problems, it often went unidentified because of its characterization as a spiritual, moral and social issue. Despite Wayne Wheeler's attempt to fill Congress with members elected by grass-roots coalitions formed by mainstream America, for the most part the old ruling class still ruled. They still had the best educations, the most money and the best connections. Prohibition had forced some of them into a disturbing hypocrisy where they sounded Dry but drank as much as ever behind closed doors.

Pauline Sabin was a member of this privileged class of easterners. She was the daughter of a former secretary of the navy, granddaughter of a former secretary of agriculture and wife of a bank president. She, like millions of other women, had been lured into voting Dry by Wheeler's images of an alcohol-free and therefore trouble-free America, where young men and women could grow up without fear of addiction. She was among the first in her circle to realize that the Volstead Act was having a paradoxical effect. More people than ever, especially young ones, were frequenting speakeasies, getting addicted, going to jail. She spoke of her concerns privately at first, among her friends and relatives in New York and Chicago, but much more would follow.

Chapter 7

FOXES IN HENHOUSES

SHERIFF STECKTER

Immediately after the raid at Dago Mary's, Sheriff Joe Harris drove to Chiles Valley and arrested his own brother, Harry Harris, who was working as a laborer at the Sievers Winery (site of today's Volker Eisele Winery) and also bootlegged. While this may have disrupted relationships in the Harris family, it certainly proved that Joe was a highly principled lawman, and in the chaos of the 1920s, this was somewhat reassuring. Frequent news stories about Volstead crimes among elected officials revealed that corruption was eating away at the infrastructure of governments both local and national. As November 1926 drew near and the county was gearing up for elections, Joe prepared to run again. He was fifty-two and at the height of a stressful career. Then, unexpectedly, he suddenly withdrew his name from the ballot for reasons of health. This was a shocker. No one emerged right away to run for the position. Perhaps no one was prepared to lose as many friends in support of a law that had brought ruin to so many in the Napa Valley. (Harris passed away in April 1929.)

The man who finally stepped into the post was Undersheriff John "Jack" Steckter. Steckter's parents had been farming land in Oakville since the Gold Rush and were among the very first residents of that part of the county. His mother, who lived to be 103, once reminisced about the many Wappo

Indians who used to live near the family ranch, long since gone. It's likely that the Steckters grew grapes at least part of the time.

Steckter conducted no raids at all for several months, even when Dave and Nellie Cavagnaro ran an ad in the newspaper about a big meeting of the Italian Catholic Federation at the couple's Brooklyn Hotel. In addition to the ravioli and the roast chicken, it said, beer would be "extra." More than three hundred people attended, but no squad cars showed up. The Cavagnaros served alcohol at their bar throughout Prohibition and, other than the Dago Mary's incident, were never arrested for it. When business was slow, Dave would actually hide the hooch and arrange for a raid to drum up some publicity. He was not the only source of alcohol in Napa. Old-timers tell of businesses near the river that had trapdoors that would deposit bottles in the river if it became necessary to get rid of evidence quickly.

When federal agents came to town in April 1927, arrests picked up. Under the direction of the feds, Sheriff Steckter and Police Chief Hewitt apprehended F.A. Nussberger of the Napa Hotel and another man, James Hanrahan, for bootlegging. Each was fined only $200. Steckter organized another raid in June that nailed four Yountville farmers: Tom Mitchell, William Edington, Allen Halter and Bruce March. Although they were fined $500 each, they only had to pay $50. In July, Calistoga constable Pierce arrested a local woman named McConnell when her still blew up in her chicken coop and they found three hundred gallons of mash, ten gallons of brandy and a pile of labels that said, "Gordon Gin, Made in London." A reader of the *Napa Journal* wrote that paper on July 7, 1927, and complained that the woman had been distilling her concoction for at least a year and that the operation was backed "by parties in this community who have money, not the poor fool who got caught. And who did the catching? Not the Sheriff nor the District Attorney. This bunch have not, nor do they want to catch this bootlegger gang." Steckter responded by going to Yountville and arresting, over the next three weeks, twelve more people there with no apparent connection to Mrs. McConnell's chicken coop.

There were those who believed that Jack Steckter was involved in a bootlegging ring that included Judge King and the DA, Wally Rutherford, both of whom liked to drink. The grand jury was investigating something, and the lid seemed about to blow, especially when John Walden, editor of the *Napa Daily Journal*, began printing dark references to problems in high places and Steckter's failure to enforce Volstead laws. When the explosion came, it appeared to have nothing to do with bootlegging. The coroner/ public administrator, William Blake, was caught misappropriating assets and was removed from office. For whatever reason, Walden resigned from the *Journal* the next day, and Judge Percy King's son became the interim editor. He would win no Pulitzer Prizes. "Those in charge of the investigation," he wrote, "ask that nothing be said." There were plenty of people who believed that Blake was thrown to the wolves to satisfy bloodlust on the part of suspicious Napans, while concealing a much larger problem than the theft of small articles from the dead. Blake never recovered from the incident; he committed suicide six months later, leaving a wife and three children.

Dishonesty on the part of Prohibition agents was a problem throughout the United States, and it included everything from simple errors like arrests and seizures in the absence of search warrants, as the Mastalattos had done, to extortion, to murder. A Napa woman (Mabelle Bush) working for the State Narcotics Division, a section of the Prohibition Department, became embroiled in a wicked controversy. She claimed to have discovered a widespread ring of corruption emanating from within the department itself. When she threatened to blow the whistle, her superiors told her they would reveal her amorous affair with a small-time criminal, thereby ruining her reputation and ensuring she would never work in Sacramento again. Both sides did as they had advertised. The chief of the Narcotics Division declined to comment on Miss Bush's charges. The governor said he would look into the situation fully, but a few days later, he changed his mind. The work of the department, he said, was to rehabilitate the addicted; it could never be involved in something as unsavory as the morally questionable Miss Bush had insinuated.

The opportunity for temptation was greatest for the officers charged with arresting malfeasants. Acceptance of bribes and improper confiscation of evidence were commonplace all across the country. When Herman Peterman of Napa's Russ House was busted for selling alcohol, the arresting agent failed to show up in court. Peterman's lawyer, Frank Silva, discovered that the agent had been caught accepting a $10,000 bribe in a case in Sonoma County and had fled the country. There was also the matter of those thousands of dollars collected in fines. The under-budgeted Prohibition Department lacked enough auditors to monitor the monies involved in each case tried before a judge or commissioner.

Although Napans entertained themselves with whispers of a bootlegging ring among the city's highest officials, corruption at that level never came to light. Bootlegging in the Napa Valley continued, of course. The fire department had its hands full dealing with exploding stills, especially in Italian Town. The air was often thick with the smell of burning tires, a ruse to conceal the tang of distillation. Grapes still grew and the juice still fermented. Some whose winemaking skills were no longer needed for legal activities employed them for illegal ones, doing custom work for wealthy patrons. They stored the fermenting product in enclosures all over the valley until it was ready to sell.

Not all incriminating evidence was easy to hide. Stills, especially large ones, could be bulky. When he heard that Undersheriff Gaffney was coming to raid his still, Joe Tiran, an Oakville farmer, dismantled it and tried to conceal it under a haystack. Gaffney found it, along with forty gallons of brandy and two thousand gallons of wine.

Another form of personal bootlegging also occurred in the Napa Valley. Longtime St. Helena resident Stella Raymond described how some local residents signed up for regular deliveries of jugs of alcoholic brew. The bootlegger—perhaps someone like her father, Albert Galli, a truck driver—would hide a filled jug under the elevated front steps of private clients' homes, accessed by a specially built little door; he would remove whatever empty bottles he found there, just like the milkman did, and replace them with filled ones. With their background in bringing wine to thirsty miners, Nichelini family members continued to provide a similar service for selected customers. Bill Nichelini, Sunny Jim's friend, had a distribution company and drove shipments of sacramental wine for Beaulieu and Beringer's. Unholy Nichelini products found their way onto and off his truck of holy wines.

In interviewing longtime Napa Valley residents about their experiences during Prohibition, historian William Heintz found that even in the 1970s and '80s, when the interviews were conducted, many of his subjects were afraid to admit their family's involvement in bootlegging, although there were quite a few who said "everyone bootlegged." It is clear that scores of residents, especially men from Switzerland and Northern Italy, augmented their meager incomes with illegal sales of alcohol. Members of the Pocai, Poggi, Rossi, Domingos, Fagiani and Pelissa families were just a few who were said to bootleg wine without getting caught. The 1930 U.S. Census reveals the heart of their problem. In the column listing "occupation," row after row of Napa County citizens wrote "none."

ESCALATION

When Jack Steckter finally starting making Volstead arrests, he focused on the sad tatters of Yountville. He and his men apprehended dozens of Yountvillains, not only for alcohol violations but now for drug-related offenses as well. He confiscated 160 cubes of morphine and some hypodermic needles from someone named Merle Meyers in Yountville in 1928. Merle was described as a major supplier for the area. Steckter brought in repeat offender Andy Zadrow so many times on alcohol and drug charges that it was hard to find a jury to try him. He finally got sent to state prison for a long stay.

The use of banned substances was very much on the rise throughout America, and men and women were both consuming them. This was the age of the flapper: the young, sexually liberated woman who wore her hair and her skirt short, used makeup, listened to jazz in formerly forbidden parts of town, smoked and drove a flivver. The Nineteenth Amendment had given her the right to vote; she was now equal to men and could go to the same poorly lit places her date or husband frequented, smoke cigarettes and sip the same illegal brew. Speakeasies and jazz clubs replaced saloons, which tolled the death knell to many houses of ill fame. Prostitution was a male-only service. The presence of women changed everything. Dressed in feathers and beads, women could dance until they dropped.

Some did, but it wasn't always the dancing that felled them. The WCTU reported that the death rate from alcohol poisoning and poisoned alcohol was forty times greater by the last years of the 1920s than it had been at the start of the decade. Alcohol caused the death of several people in the Napa Valley during Prohibition, and the beleaguered town of Yountville saw more than its share of these. Some were the result of tempers enflamed by booze. Two drunken old vets named John at the home got into a spat about a set of false teeth in 1928. One John stabbed the other to death over them. A few months later, someone brought five gallons of liquor to a surreptitious party at the home. It was poisonous and killed three people, including the chief dietician. These deaths were the direct result of a misguided intervention by the federal government. To force the makers of industrial alcohol to produce a product people couldn't consume, the federal government required them to include a poisonous additive. People like the Veterans Home group drank it anyway and died or went blind. Death by lead was also on the upswing. Shootings among rival gang members in places like Chicago made exciting, if scary, reading.

Perhaps because Napa County's Volstead numbers were slipping, the Treasury Department sent men to conduct some well-placed raids. They incensed the east Napa community by nabbing Louis "Bonnie" Rossi, a decorated World War I hero who received the *croix de guerre* for spending two days in the heat of battle repairing communication cables for the Allied armies. The agents destroyed 1,300 gallons of wine in Rossi's possession. As with George Blaufuss, Judge King stepped in to exact the fine: $200. The Bommarito brothers of St. Helena did not enjoy the same good fortune. The federal judge in San Francisco, Frank Kerrigan, sentenced them to six months each for operating a still. He stipulated that while one brother was serving time, the other could manage their vineyard, and that at the end of the first brother's term they could switch places.

Friends often helped friends pay their fines. The postmaster of tiny Pope Valley, Thomas Neil, sold two shots of whiskey to federal agents, who discovered that he also had on his premises two gallons of wine and a gallon of whiskey. He was jailed. Henry Conner and Ralph Dollarhide contributed the $2,000 it took to bail him out.

Meanwhile, the state Supreme Court, which had been deliberating the legality of impounding Nathan Ghisolfo's wine in Calistoga, finally rendered its decision. The court agreed with Ghisolfo that he had committed no offense and returned his wine to him. This landmark ruling resulted in millions of gallons of improperly confiscated alcoholic beverages being reunited with their creators. It also included language that required agents to use due process when seizing or otherwise impounding the property of American citizens. Lawyers could now defend their clients by having cases thrown out of court for procedural flaws.

The Ghisolfo decision revealed waning enthusiasm on the part of some key government officials for Wayne Wheeler's once gloried Prohibition juggernaut. Wheeler himself suffered a horrible reversal of fortune that could have been scripted in Hollywood. In August 1927, he, his wife, Ella, and her parents went to a lake in Michigan to enjoy some R&R at a rustic cottage. Emma's father, Robert Candy, was recovering from a heart attack, and Wayne, who also had heart problems, desperately needed a vacation. While Ella was working in the kitchen, a large drum of gasoline that had been placed near the stove somehow exploded, setting her clothes on fire. She ran into the living room screaming. Her father leaped from his couch, clutched his chest and keeled over dead. Emma died the next day from her burns. Wheeler appeared to take these tragedies in stride, but three weeks later, his own heart failed and it was he who toppled over, dead.

Another Methodist, Bishop James Cannon, took Wheeler's place at the helm of the ASL. Cannon was a Virginia Democrat with pronounced anti-Catholic and racist beliefs that were common to his time and place, as well as a sneaky side.

HOOVER V. SMITH

The 1928 election pitted a Wet Catholic urban Democrat, Al Smith, against a Dry Protestant more-or-less rural Republican, Herbert Hoover. James Cannon fled the Democrats and backed Hoover. Mabel Willebrandt, a feisty and effective assistant attorney general who succeeded Annette Adams, also backed Hoover, and to prove her point that Smith was a known drinker, she orchestrated Volstead raids on the night of his nomination, an event that was also greeted by a rim of fire around the convention hall in Houston, courtesy of the KKK.

Hoover won the 1928 election easily, and the Republicans understood his victory as a mandate to further strengthen Prohibition laws. The defeat of Smith led "Bone Dry" senator Morris Sheppard of Texas to proclaim, "Prohibition is forever anchored in the head and purpose of Almighty God!" Sheppard was mistaken. The anchor was actually lodged in the same xenophobia that had long plagued mainstream America. Catholics, Jews and southern blacks continued to migrate into the strongholds of the traditional majority. With no insight into the fact that the nation's craze to be Dry was cooling down, Herbert Hoover used his inaugural address to castigate those who defied the Eighteenth Amendment. Defiance of Volstead laws, he warned, undermined all other laws as well. Accordingly, he immediately took measures to increase Prohibition-related enforcement and punishments.

The ASL's Cannon worked with a senator from the state of Washington, Wesley Jones, to devise a legal tourniquet to torture Wets into compliance. The Jones Law defined all Volstead violations as felonies (not misdemeanors, which most had been), demanded prison terms of one year plus a fine of $10,000 for first offenders and ascribed equal guilt to purchasers of liquor and witnesses to purchases. Offenders who couldn't afford to pay their fines would be required to work in prison at the rate of $1 a day until their accounts were settled. Lodged somewhere among the spikes and daggers was a stipulation that heads of households would no longer be allowed to make two hundred gallons of wine, beer or booze for their own enjoyment.

Assistant Attorney General Mabel Willebrandt was not responsible for having to enforce any of these draconian measures. For her assiduous dedication to prosecuting on behalf of the Eighteenth Amendment, she expected to be named attorney general, but Hoover selected someone else. She resigned.

With Hoover in office and the feds revving up their enforcement, Dave Cavagnaro feared he might not get the same degree of protection he had enjoyed in the past, especially since Punch, his trusty informant, had gone to Sacramento to take a job with the Department of Motor Vehicles. Dave packed his bag, kissed his wife goodbye and joined the circus.

Socialite Pauline Sabin had seen and heard enough of Hoover as well. Sending impoverished offenders to a kind of debtor's prison was cruel and unusual, she believed. The implication that her friends, most of whom still liked their scotches and dry martinis, were subverting the entire rule of law in the United States was ridiculous. It was Prohibition itself that made no sense, and the Jones Law was a monstrosity. She quit her position on the Republican National Committee, gathered a group of trusted female friends and led the establishment of the Women's Organization for National Prohibition Reform. Her coterie included Mrs. August Belmont, Mrs. William Draper, Mrs. Pierre du Pont, Mrs. Caspar Whitney and Mrs. Archibald Roosevelt, along with other determined women from powerful families. Many of their children, grandchildren and great-grandchildren would eventually live in a much-transformed Napa Valley.

An alliance to repeal the Volstead Act had been in place for several years: the Association Against the Prohibition Amendment. Industrialist Pierre du Pont was among its early supporters. Like Sabin, he had been swayed at the outset by the thought of a nation without alcohol abuse, but he, too, observed the tyrannies that had evolved in the attempt to enforce abstention. With the help of his former bookkeeper and financial whiz J.J. Raskob, he pulled in a number of business leaders. Decades later, Raskob, a Catholic philanthropist, would be a major donor in the creation of Queen of the Valley Hospital in Napa.

Throughout the 1928 presidential campaign, the nation had been bombarded by opinion, not only in the usual form of propaganda by leaflet but in a new way as well: radio. According to one source (xroads.virginia.edu), an astounding 60 percent of American households bought radios during the 1920s after the first commercial broadcast, which took place in 1920. As now, "talk radio" was capable of stirring up listeners' negative emotions. The KKK thrived. Conspiracy theories involving the pope and fables of atrocities committed by Catholics (aka "Papists") abounded, foreshadowing the anti-Semitic broadcasts in Nazi Germany that were soon to follow. It would be decades, however, before historians could appreciate the dynamics that were actually at work. Protestants and Catholics spat insults at each other on the airwaves and in print, but historians today seem to agree that when it came to diatribes, anti-Catholic/nativistic sentiment dominated. (See, for example, *Prejudice and the Old Politics*, by Alan Lichtman, 2000.)

Throughout the decade, hard liquor, which was easier to get and store than wine, became the substance of choice for millions of Americans who were growing weary of the federal government telling them how to run their lives. The money for the alcohol-sodden adventures of the 1920s flowed as abundantly as the booze itself. In most places, the economy was enjoying a boom that exceeded that of the 1880s. The '20s may have begun that way for growers of wine grapes, but in 1928, the bottom fell out of the grape market. Napa Valley viticulturalists like Charles Forni suddenly had no buyers. Wine was just too much trouble for most people to make, especially when bottles of scotch and gin were tumbling across the Canadian border by the trainload.

The Treasury Department had gotten suspicious about what buyers were doing with the grapes Forni and his friends were shipping to Chicago. They prepared a questionnaire for consignees of grape shipments to fill out. Al Capone preempted the T-men by having some of his own people pose as Treasury agents with forms for buyers. The frightened consignees abandoned the grapes at the train yard, allowing Capone to steal the entire load.

Or so the story went. Al Capone's name had become a household word, and to many, he was the wily fox who eluded the government's hounds and thus a kind of dark hero. Violence among gang members made grisly, if captivating, reading, to the point where names like Lucky Luciano and Bugsy Moran were also household words, striking no admiration but lots of fear. While it was mainly at this element that the over-the-top Jones Law aimed, it raised the stakes for ordinary bootleggers and resulted in an escalation of violence at the local level. This violence made its way to the Napa Valley.

One family to feel the chill of this new reality was that of Virgil and Angele Galleron, who lived three miles south of St. Helena. One day in March 1928, two men with guns showed up at their door and asked to buy wine. Virgil said they didn't have any. The men then declared that they were federal agents, and one of them flashed a badge. They forced their way in. Angele ran to the kitchen and telephoned the police, and the men fled.

At the very end of 1929, a federal agent fittingly named Jones bought alcohol from a Yountville couple, the Souths. He obtained an arrest warrant from Commissioner Palmer and brought another officer, Robert Freeman, back to the Souths to arrest them. The place seemed deserted when they returned. They browsed through the kitchen cabinets and found numerous bottles of booze, which they set on the counter. There was a shed in the back, which they set out to investigate; when they returned to the kitchen, they found John South pouring the liquor down the drain. South and Freeman began to fight, and as they fell to the floor, South grabbed a gun from the shelf and fired, but the shot went wild. Jones sped to the kitchen brandishing his riot club. South fired again, but Freeman forced his arm up and the shot whizzed past Jones's head. Jones raised the club to bash South and felt a steely jab in his spine. It was Grace South with a double-barreled shotgun. "If you hit him, I'll kill you," she said.

John South scrambled to his feet and discharged a third time, just as Jones wheeled around and knocked the weapon out of Grace's hands. It, too, went off, sending shot into the wood-burning stove. Robert Freeman clutched his chest. "I'm hit," he gasped. "Let's get out of here."

Jones drove the bleeding Freeman to the hospital at the Veterans Home just a few blocks away. They lacked the means to help him, so he was transported to the brand-new Victory Hospital on Jefferson Street in Napa. Surgeons found a .25-caliber bullet—John South's—in his lung. He died within a few days, and John South was charged with murder. He was found guilty and sentenced to ten years in prison.

Another death in 1929 also caught the attention of people in the Napa Valley. At least this one wasn't in Yountville; it was in Oakville, just a few miles up the road. The airport at the old Doak place was doing very well, but the McGill/Doak family was not. Frieda Doak McGill's daughter Elizabeth (D. Perry Doak's stepdaughter) had developed an intense dislike for the army colonel. She had been heard muttering that she wished John McGill were dead. The reasons why she felt this way were never revealed, but her wish was granted. One evening during happy hour, he took a sip of his cocktail, began foaming at the mouth and collapsed. When the authorities arrived, Betty was merrily playing the piano and singing in the same room where the corpse was stiffening. Sheriff Steckter never arrested Elizabeth Doak. McGill's death was not ruled foul play, but Elizabeth herself may have been the victim of crimes perpetrated by McGill. She went on to have five failed marriages and finally took her own life.

In fact, much of what was happening in the country was hard to swallow. Hoover had ascended to power on a bubble that burst in October 1929. By the end of 1930, banks, farms and manufacturers started to fail. An immediate effect of this was a startling rise in unemployment. Because there was no system of social security, no government agency could help the jobless. The suicide rate spiked. Quite a few occurred in Napa County. The manufacture, transportation and sale of illegal beverages continued. Bootlegging was one way for the desperate to put food on the table. As it always had, consumption of the bootlegger's wares provided temporary relief from the miseries of everyday life but lured increasing numbers of people into an ever-deepening abyss.

Federal agents continued to target Napans. They arrested Joe Tamburelli yet again and accused him of "conducting a nuisance" at his Depot Restaurant, but when the case came to trial, the agents were unable to establish that Tamburelli actually sold alcohol there. It was the agents who were the nuisance. They also hauled in Demetrio Scaruffi and Anecito Negri—the usual suspects.

GRAPE BRICKS

What little life remained in the Napa Valley wine industry flickered near to extinction in 1930. But not quite. Beaulieu, with its business in altar wines, was still doing all right. Sacramental wine also kept Beringer's in business, but just barely, and the winery began selling off portions of its land to scrape by. The Beringers hit upon a clever idea. They had installed a fruit dehydrator to dry their grapes, and they started using it to create "grape bricks"—blocks of dried grapes that, if submerged in a gallon of water with a pound of sugar, would, under the proper conditions, make wine. They sold the bricks with warnings to avoid leaving the ingredients in warm places for too long, lest fermentation occur. The Treasury Department didn't approve of grape bricks, but it didn't prosecute the Beringers either.

In fact, the concept caught on. A cooperative of growers—mainly raisin growers in the Central Valley—called themselves Fruit Industries and created something they called Vine Glo based on the identical recipe. The Bank of Italy (soon-to-be Bank of America) funded their enterprise and ran an ad in the *Napa Journal* in June 1930 proclaiming that "In Unity There Is Strength." But when the disastrous stock market plunge and its prolonged aftermath finally impacted that financial giant as well, it could no longer back Fruit Industries. Vine Glo's organizers turned to the federal government, specifically the newly created national Farm Board, for help and hired a lawyer with special

Bertha Beringer was the force behind the survival of her family's winery. She marketed "grape bricks" for do-it-yourself vintners. *Courtesy of Walt and Geri Raymond.*

experience in Prohibition law to represent and advocate for them: former Assistant Attorney General Mabel Willebrandt. With her name and the stamp of approval of a government agency, Vine Glo did very well for a year or two. When a St. Louis–based company tried to start up a grape brick business to compete with Vine Glo, the federal government charged it with violating the Volstead Act. The Hoover administration seemed to be conceding that people did, in fact, like to drink alcoholic products occasionally and that the wine industry had been correct in its argument that wine was less destructive than hard liquor or beer and the saloons that served it. But rather than resurrecting privately run wineries, the government would go into the wine business itself.

Hoover established the Farm Board in order to stabilize the price of agricultural products. Farming all across the country had fallen into the black hole of the Great Depression along with most other industries. As a branch of the Farm Bureau, Fruit Industries organized a Grape Control Board to dictate the price of grapes in California. To help set the price, it determined how much tonnage should be harvested, and to ensure that the numbers remained predictable, Fruit Industries agreed to recruit at least 85 percent of all the grape growers in the state. No grapes at all were to go directly to consumers. Most Napa Valley farmers had their own ideas about what they wanted to grow and resisted the Grape Control Board, but in the end, some signed on.

The legal and illegal wine business both had cause for concern. With the Jones Law in effect, the personal wine allotment loophole of two hundred gallons had closed. Growers like Charles Forni were suddenly without customers. Beaulieu would be in trouble too if this trend continued. There would be no need for privately produced altar wine if the government made it or sold Vine Glo; parishes could turn their own water into wine. Al Capone was in a snit; if people could make their wine from Vine Glo, it would cut into an important aspect of his empire. From his point of view,

Theodore Gier's Sequoia in the hills west of Napa became the Christian Brothers' Mont La Salle. *Courtesy of the Napa Valley Wine Library Association.*

the grape growers of Fruit Industries had betrayed him. In November 1930, he sent word to his aides to "wage war" with anyone in Napa County who did business with Fruit Industries. There could be "a few deaths," he hissed. Nothing happened in the Napa Valley, but elsewhere there were tales of cars being driven off the road by thugs, reminiscent of the fate of Theodore Bell.

With his hefty fines and other financial woes, the other Theodore whose life had changed drastically with Prohibition, Theodore Gier, could no longer support his remaining vineyard, Sequoia, on Mount Veeder (now the Hess Collection). He sold it in 1930 to Christian Brothers, who had been making sacramental wine in Martinez. Like Beaulieu, Christian Brothers' alcohol endeavors had been doing fairly well throughout Prohibition. (It sold eighty thousand barrels of wine in 1925, for example.) The Martinez facility, Villa de La Salle, had easy access to railroad lines, and to discourage theft, they transported their wine in barrels of flour. They tore down some of Gier's buildings, ferried their equipment across the Carquinez Strait, built a new facility and renamed Gier's place Mont La Salle. They continued to conceal their output in flour barrels, these labeled now as "Mont La Salle Products."

The brothers' Napa neighbors, like Gier, were bootlegging. William and Henry Brandlin owned a ranch on Redwood Road, adjacent to the Christian Brothers' new facility. The feds found an enormous still there with fifty-five thousand gallons of mash and two trucks loaded with hooch. The facility boasted cutting-edge technology that featured an electric-powered distiller that could churn out six hundred gallons daily. Harry Attebury, a twenty-six-year-old Napan, was identified as the brains behind the operation. A team of eight officers caught ten men there in the process of manufacturing illicit beverages and identified Brandlin Ranch as a major supplier for the Bay Area. The man who sold the motors that ran the assembly line, G. Fleuti, eventually found his way to jail as well.

Remote Loveall Valley was not far away, straddling the Napa/Sonoma border. It was the site of two busts. The first netted $35,000 worth of equipment, 40,000 gallons of alcohol and 40,000 pounds of sugar for future productions but apparently no bootleggers. Two federal agents, Buckley and Morgue, returned a few months later and found signs that the operation had started up again. They hid in the brush and waited. While Buckley warded off the evening chill by sipping the contents of a flask he had brought with him, a truck with two men rumbled up the trail leading to the still. One man sat in the cab and drove while the other straddled some sacks of sugar in the flatbed. The one in the cab saw the agents, pulled out a rifle and shot at them. Buckley returned fire and hit the man in the flatbed, who fell from the truck with a bullet in his stomach. Buckley then picked up the wounded man and used him as a shield while firing at the driver until he grazed him in the head and he surrendered. The raid uncovered a huge copper still and 100,000 gallons of corn whiskey. At the hearing that followed, Morgue told the coroner's jury that Buckley had been drinking just before the shooting began, which ended Buckley's career.

Chapter 8

REPEAL

ECLIPSE OF AN INDUSTRY

Vine Glo did not thrive. The federal government's entrance into the wine business faltered because wine itself was failing as a commodity of choice among Americans, regardless of their religion or ethnicity. Booze was so much easier to get. The market for personal winemaking was dead; the only place most Americans were drinking wine was in church. If Thomas Jefferson, George Crane and others were right and wine actually was a "temperance" drink of sorts, the alcohol-consuming sector of America was at risk of falling into a dangerous and chronic intemperance.

Herbert Hoover never put much energy into promoting research for alcoholism, but he did commission an eleven-member blue ribbon panel to investigate and provide suggestions for a solution to the soaring crime rate. After many months of study, the Wickersham Commission concluded that police tactics tended to be too harsh and that corruption was rampant. People all over the country continued to drink on the sly, and their local governments were too protective of them, they found. Much more aggressive law enforcement was needed, they said, with more agents and a bigger bureaucracy to support them. The prospect of hiring the hundreds of additional agents necessary to enforce the unpopular law was difficult for some to accept, but Hoover did it anyway.

The Wickersham Report did nothing to help Hoover's public relations. Neither did the ominous weather. A severe drought began in 1930 and continued throughout '31 and '32. (It would last for several more years.) Crops were failing. Stocks of Transamerica, the holding company for the Bank of Italy/Bank of America, hit an all-time low.

Hoover continued to believe that governmental control of prices and a more powerful Treasury Department would help turn things around. The House obediently voted an additional $11 million for Prohibition enforcement, raising the budget for that branch of the government to $44 million for 1931. To facilitate the more severe policing he wanted, Hoover moved Prohibition enforcement from the Treasury Department to the Department of Justice.

The personal income tax made possible by the Seventeenth Amendment was not nearly enough for the federal government's needs, especially with the nation in an economic crisis. Nevertheless, Hoover wanted to reduce the income tax by 1 percent so the wealthy, most of whom lost money in the stock market crash of 1929, would have more money to spend, as if that would mend the nation's woes. He finally realized that would cure nothing and ended up raising income taxes instead. To protect favored industries, he also asked for a greater tariff on imports, which increased the cost of nonnative goods. American trading partners responded by raising their tariffs on U.S. exports. Some of his own supporters began to count the cost of the revenue that had been lost because of the Volstead Act. In October 1930, a Prohibition spokesman revealed that if the bootleg liquor that had been rounded up since 1920 had been taxed, it would have brought in $8,763,387,180 a year.

The cracks that were spreading under the paint of the Drys' mighty coalition may not have been immediately apparent, but they were there. A National Prohibition Referendum Association formed and immediately collected signatures of twenty thousand people wanting the future of the Eighteenth Amendment to be brought to vote. The popular *Literary Digest* magazine polled twenty million Americans to see how they felt about Prohibition laws. The majority said they were unhappy with them.

HOOVER V. ROOSEVELT

Franklin D. Roosevelt would oppose Hoover in the 1932 election. FDR had been open in his criticism of Prohibition, as were increasing numbers of

Some bought special license plates to advertise their opinion about Prohibition. The bell insignia on the upper corners honors Theodore Bell.

his aristocratic friends, including Republican ones and even Republicans who themselves did not drink, like John D. Rockefeller. Spokesmen for the formerly Dry California Grange also urged members to vote for repeal if the opportunity arose. Labor unions in California concurred: the saloons should continue to be outlawed, but the Eighteenth Amendment should be repealed. The American Federation of Labor, American Bar Association, American Medical Association and American Legion all came out against Prohibition as it currently stood.

Socialite Pauline Sabin's reading of the national temperament was clearer than Hoover's or the Wickersham Committee's. Her Women's Organization for National Prohibition Reform, officially organized in 1929, had become a major political force by 1931. Sabin deplored the intrusion of government into the personal choices of adults and observed that the romance of speakeasies and wily bootleggers was actually leading more young people into alcoholism than ever before, while encouraging organized crime. Women from all classes, but especially the wealthy, continued to join her in her personal crusade against Prohibition. Pierre du Pont and J.J. Raskob's Association Against the Prohibition of Alcohol also grew in strength, drawing similar numbers of men.

They threatened to publish (but didn't) a list of senators and congressmen who voted Dry but lived Wet. There were plenty of them.

A group of New York attorneys calling themselves the Voluntary Committee of Lawyers analyzed the mechanics of repealing or radically revising the Eighteenth Amendment and spoke to members of Congress. They learned that only 145 signatures would be needed to revise the amendment to a "home rule" option, where individual states could decide whether they wanted to be Wet or Dry. A bipartisan group got together to consider the option of allowing "light wine" and low-alcohol beer and setting up a government-run system of dispensing them. Sixty-four Republicans abandoned the Dry cause in December 1931 and joined the Wets in supporting light beer.

COLLAPSE OF A MOVEMENT

Discrediting facts about ASL leader Wayne Wheeler's successor, James Cannon, surfaced that fed a mounting distaste toward the Dry movement. It came out, for example, that just before grain and sugar were rationed to support the war, Cannon had purchased large amounts of these two commodities and hid them. He sold them on the black market during the war for great profit. He was also involved in some shady stock market deals and had a clandestine love affair. In the summer of 1930, he fled the country with his new wife to become a missionary in Brazil. This did not sit well with the Methodist Church. He was asked to return to the United States and respond to some serious questions.

But even if Cannon had been a saint, and even if the weather had been better, and even if the Wickersham Committee hadn't gone public with its contradictory and inflammatory report, it is likely that Prohibition would have run aground. The crime it had engendered was the Volstead Act's most obvious side effect. It was also clear that financial chaos had enveloped the country, and revenue from alcohol-related taxes was no longer available to staunch the flow. Other important but less obvious factors were also at play to weaken the fervor that had ushered in Prohibition back in the 'teens.

- The beer-brewing, saloonkeeping Germans had been defeated in the Great War. Anti-Teutonic propaganda no longer filled mailboxes. (Although the caustic split between Protestants and Catholics continued.)

- The influenza virus had mutated into a kinder, gentler form, so bargains with God linking health with abstinence were no longer necessary.
- Women had the vote. Complaints about male fondness for alcohol had subsided. Indeed, more women were now drinking than ever before. Florence Kahn, a U.S. congresswoman from San Francisco, made news when she denounced Prohibition on a live radio show in October 1930. Kahn was a widow who took over when her husband died in office unexpectedly. She was a role model for many women who could now turn their political energy into positive directions.
- Wayne Wheeler was dead, and the appeal of the ASL as well as the WCTU was fading fast. Contributions to these two once powerful organizations dried to a trickle. James Cannon's replacement, Scott McBride, conceded that Hoover might not win by a landslide as he had against Al Smith. He set about preparing speakers and pamphlets in Hoover's support, but lacking the private donations that had made it possible, the ASL was virtually silenced.

Without the cultural underpinnings that produced it, support for the Eighteenth Amendment fell like a house of cards.

Meanwhile, with added support from the federal Department of Justice, alcohol raids in the Napa Valley continued. Longtime Napa saloon men C.L. Carbone and Charles Townsend were arrested for selling beer. The bar at Carbone's Napa Hotel was a soda fountain at the time of the sting; Townsend had been a bartender. Wine was found at the Genoa Hotel. The malfeasants were released on their own recognizance. Carbone was busted again a few months later for the same offense.

Federal agents smelled fermentation in Rutherford and traced it to a still on the R.E. Wood ranch in Rutherford. As with the Brandlin Ranch, they found cutting-edge equipment there but no personnel. Farmer Pete Granzella, already suffering from financial problems with three sons and two daughters, got caught with parts of a still on his property. Despairing, he shot himself.

In February 1932, Sheriff Steckter resumed his harassment of Yountville. He raided five "liquor resorts" on what was being characterized as Yountville's "liquor row": the Stone House (James Forrester), the Hole in the Ground (William Cohen), the Magnolia Hotel (Harry Avery), the Veterans Sport Club (Robert Smith) and the Yountville Grocery Store (Henry Lavelle). A few weeks later, he and Undersheriff Gaffney busted the Camille Ceriani family in Brown's Valley for possessing two thousand gallons of wine—their second offense—and Manuel Santos, a Portuguese dairyman in Dry Creek, for having four hundred gallons. Another swoop into Yountville caught Philip Merino and William Ellis. Demetrio Scaruffi, whom they had targeted previously, was caught with wine and beer on his Third Street premises in Napa, as was a Mrs. Rush, also on Third, who had beer. Arrests for these relatively small offenses proliferated, and they angered people, but with so many extra federal agents around, local sheriff's departments were unable to look the other way. In other parts of the country, similar raids were prompting citizens to riot. Young Charles Ceriani was arrested that summer in Sonoma for shooting a gun from his car at passing vehicles—an expression, perhaps, of personal rage at the world in general for the unfairness of it all.

In addition to causing propagating pain for the arrested, publicizing Prohibition arrests alerted outsiders to the idea that forbidden substances might be found at certain places. After the 1932 bust of the Yountville Grocery Store, three armed men showed up there in a large sedan, brandishing guns. Proprietor Henry Lavelle dropped behind the counter and drew his own weapon. They ran off and drove around the corner, firing two shots at him. He fired back, wounding one in the process. A patron named Frank Peres hopped in his car and tried to chase them down, but they got away. A bullet was found lodged in the outside wall, near where Lavelle had been standing.

Prohibition commissioner James Palmer, no champion of the Dry cause, was inundated with cases. He could not help but be aware of the financial damage so many Volstead fines were doing to so many local men and women. When A.R. Negri appeared before him yet again in April 1932, Palmer only fined him and his associate Peter Traverso $150.

In St. Helena, Louis Vasconi, who was still living in the family home on Madrona Avenue with his pharmacist brother Mario, his mother Luiza and Captain Gaetano Rossi, had become a justice of the peace and then a judge. Like Palmer, he ruled on Volstead cases, and he was no friend of Prohibition either. He, too, imposed minimal fines. When Pietro Viviani and Harry Donaldson were caught with 5,100 gallons of wine and 220 gallons of whiskey in their Rutherford store, he only charged them $150. The feds brought in Joe Baldocchi (a second offender, at least) for possessing a small quantity of alcohol, and Vasconi fined him $50. At the same time, the T-men caught former vintner Joseph Butala with 4,000 gallons of wine, some brandy, some beer and a still in the vineyard near his house. He went to jail on a $15,000 bond. When a pro-repeal group formed in the upper valley, Vasconi invited them to hold their meetings in his office.

The excessive penalties Hoover had suggested could not be enforced; people had hardly any money, especially in the upper Napa Valley, where the wine and grape industry had left a void that prunes and walnuts could not fill. Poverty created by unemployment caused jobless, penniless men all across America to pack their few possessions in bindles and roam the country seeking work of any kind. Encampments of these hoboes popped up in rural areas everywhere, including Napa County. Most of the hoboes abided by the law, but many weren't above snatching eggs from chickens or the hens themselves for a much-needed meal. Frieda McGill in Oakville distributed tents to shelter twenty-two families on her ranch. There was a camp near what is now the Trancas exit on Highway 29 and one on the Tyther Ranch in Yountville. Another between Wooden and Wild Horse Valleys gave employment to fifty men who cut trees for firewood. The wood was stored and split at the vacant Migliavacca Winery and sold to merchants in the Bay Area.

The federal raid on a ranch in Conn Valley, a wild section east of St. Helena, was enough to make almost everyone cynical about Prohibition and its enforcement in Napa County. The ranch belonged to former Napa attorney Edward Bell, the late Theodore's brother. After defending petty Prohibition criminals in Napa, Edward established a law practice in Oakland, where he did the same. A man named O'Hara farmed the Conn Valley ranch in question, and he had been a client of Edward's. In the summer of 1932, feds found an elaborate moonshine operation there with assets that included seven cars, two trucks and some fifty thousand gallons of mash and eighty-seven sacks of sugar. The agents were able to establish that the still supplied tax-free alcoholic "medicine" that was distributed at a drugstore in Emeryville. Nine "liquor depots" and joints were connected to the Conn Valley raid. The drugstore was across the street from the Emeryville Police Department, and the feds found a car parked in the police parking lot—tucked away between a squad car and an ambulance—that was loaded with moonshine from the Conn Valley still. O'Hara claimed that he had sublet the barn where the feds found the still to someone he barely knew. He had no knowledge, he said, of the shameful activity going on there. By this time Commissioner Palmer was well practiced in dealing with Napa politics. Before the matter could go to Sacramento, he told O'Hara he believed him, returned the $2,000 bond O'Hara had posted and dismissed the case!

The year 1932 may have been the darkest in American history. Almost a quarter of the population was unemployed, many of them nomads roaming the countryside for work. Crime was rampant almost everywhere. It occurred to many members of Congress that even if Roosevelt won the November election, the Constitution stipulated that he could not take office until March. The urgency of the nation's troubles demanded that inauguration come quickly. In March 1932, Congress proposed a new amendment, the Twentieth, shortening the "lame duck" period so that the changing of the guard, if it came, would commence in January. That this alteration of the Constitution passed so easily is noteworthy in many respects. The Constitution itself, once the tool of the Drys, was now being altered in a way that would benefit the Wets. Most people were sure Roosevelt would win; they couldn't wait to get rid of Hoover.

Roosevelt's victory numbers were colossal. As soon as he took office, the arrests stopped and he got to work on repealing the Eighteenth Amendment, which would require another constitutional amendment, the Twenty-first. Congress proposed it on February 20, 1933, and instead of the usual ratification by state legislature, where many Drys still reigned, it would become law through special ratifying conventions. While the states were going through the ratification process, he signed into law the Cullen-Harrison Act (March 1933), which allowed for the sale of "light beer," 3.2 percent alcohol. Wine was not included in this initial weakening of the Volstead Act. Repeal itself became law on December 5, 1933. At one minute past midnight, barkeeper Dave Cavagnaro, home from the circus, sent his son Ray to a San Francisco warehouse to pick up the first legal shipment of beer to Napa County. Happy Napans greeted his return to town with empty pitchers and mugs, and Ray dispensed it right from the truck.

Fifty-four Napa Valley wineries opened for business on December 6, but few people came to buy. Prohibition and the Great Depression it helped create destroyed most of what was once a vibrant industry. By 1962, there were only twenty-six wineries left, among them Nichelini, which is now the only surviving privately run winery in Napa County to have remained in business before, during and after Prohibition.

BIBLIOGRAPHY

BOOKS

Allen, Frederick Lewis. *The Big Change*. New York: Harper & Row, 1952.

Behr, Edward. *Thirteen Years that Changed America*. New York: Arcade Publishing, 1996.

Cashman, Sean Dennis. *Prohibition: The Lie of the Land*. New York: The Free Press, 1981.

Cleland, Robert Glass. *California in Our Time*. New York: Alfred A. Knopf, 1947.

Coffey, Thomas M. *The Long Thirst*. London: Hamish Hamilton, 1975.

Feldman, Herman. *Prohibition: Its Economic and Industrial Aspects*. New York: D. Appleton and Company, 1927.

Gentry, Curt F. *The Madams of San Francisco*. New York: Doubleday & Company, 1964.

Gregory, Thomas Jefferson. *History of Solano and Napa Counties*. Los Angeles: Historic Record Company, 1912.

Heintz, William F. *Wine Country: A History of the Napa Valley*. Santa Barbara, CA: Capra Press, 1990.

Iezzoni, Lynette. *Influenza 1918*. New York: TV Books, LLC, 1999.

Issel, William, and Robert W. Cherny. *San Francisco 1865–1932*. Berkeley: University of California Press, 1986.

Jakes, Warren, and Richard Utt. *The Vision Bold*. Washington, D.C.: Review and Herald Publishing Association, 1977.

Kerr, K. Austin. *Organized for Prohibition*. New Haven, CT: Yale University Press, 1985.

Lichtman, Allan. *Prejudice and the Old Politics*. Chapel Hill: University of North Carolina Press, 1979.

Menefee, C.A. *Historical and Descriptive Sketchbook of Napa, Sonoma, and Lake Counties*. Napa City, CA: Reporter Publishing House, 1873

Mowry, George. *The California Progressives*. Chicago: Quadrangle Books, 1963.

Okrent, Daniel. *Last Call: The Rise and Fall of Prohibition*. New York: Scribner, 2010.

Pinney, Thomas. *A History of Wine in America*. Berkeley: University of California Press, 1989.

Smith, Clarence, and Wallace Elliott. *Illustrations of Napa County California with Historical Sketch*. Oakland, CA: Smith and Elliott, 1878.

Sosnowski, Vivienne. *When the Rivers Ran Red*. New York: Palgrave MacMillan, 2009.

Sullivan, Charles. *Napa Wine*. San Francisco: Wine Appreciation Guild, 1994.

Weber, Lin. *Roots of the Present*. St. Helena, CA: Wine Ventures Publishing, 2001.

UNPUBLISHED WORKS

"History of the Napa Valley: Interviews and Reminiscences of Long-Time Residents." Vols. 1–4. St. Helena, CA: Napa Valley Wine Library Association.

Mini, Carolyn, and C. Martin. "Two Families: Cavagnaro and Guisto." Napa, CA, 1998.

Quinn, Tony. "A History of the Salmina Family of Corcapolo and St. Helena." N.p., 1994.

ARTICLES

"End of Prohibition in the United States." *Literary Digest*, November 18, 1933. www.1920-1930.com.

Evans, Richard M. "How Prohibition Was Ended." www.druglibrary.org.

Hanson, David J., PhD. "National Prohibition of Alcohol in the U.S." www2. potsdam.edu.

Husmann, George. "Grape, Raisin, and Wine Production in the United States." Yearbook of the U.S. Department of Agriculture, 1902. Washington, D.C., 1903.

Meers, John R. "The California Wine and Grape Industry and Prohibition." *California Historical Society Quarterly* 46, no. 1 (March 1967).

Sullivan, Jack. "Theodore Gier." Pre-Prowhiskeymen.blogspot.com.

WEBSITES

Ancestry.com
Cdnc.ucr.edu
En.Wikipedia.org
Etext.virginia.edu
www.napahistory.org
www.onlinebiographies.info
xroads.virginia.edu

NEWSPAPERS

Napa Daily Journal
St. Helena Star
Weekly Calistogan

INDEX

ABOUT THE AUTHOR

Prohibition in the Napa Valley: Castles Under Siege is Lin Weber's seventh history about California's world-famous wine country. She is a lifetime member of the Napa Valley Wine Library Association and the Jewish Historical Society of the Napa Valley, a former trustee of the Napa Valley Museum and a recipient of Napa Landmarks' Award of Merit. She is a licensed marriage and family therapist and an artist and has lived in the Napa Valley since 1971.

Visit us at
www.historypress.net

This title is also available as an e-book